Felt in the Jaw

Felt in the Jaw

Stories by Kristen N. Arnett

Split Lip Press

Published by Split Lip Press
333 Sinkler Road
Wyncote, PA 19095
www.splitlippress.com

ISBN: 978-01974186044

Cover Art by Alana Questell

for mattie, always

Change, when it comes, cracks everything open.

Dorothy Allison

Table of Contents

Biddenden Maids

On Bethany's bedroom wall there's a plaque that states the biblical origins of her name. It was given to her sixteen-year-old mother at a hastily thrown baby shower when Bethany was already three months old. There are pictures in an album of her mother sitting in someone's living room, swallowed up by a crowd of women nearly twice her age, clutching the plaque in one arm and a red-faced Bethany in the other. That was when her mother had still been a member of the church choir. The women had thrown her the shower and then asked her to spend more time at home.

Bethany's mother had a voice like Karen Carpenter, a husky contralto that she used when she ran the vacuum back and forth over the Oriental rug that had been in the family for three generations. Sometimes her mother had sung her name, *Beth-ah-nee*, turning the three syllables into pitches of high-low-low, the end of her name stringing out into dark velvet. Bethany can't listen to the Carpenters without thinking of her mother in a bathrobe with a rope of vacuum cord slung over her arm.

Bethany means "house of dates." It's the place where Jesus performed many miracles and spent a lot of time with his disciples. Bethany's important not because of whom it names, but what it encompasses. Not just a place or a person or even a single moment—it means multitudes. Bethany likes to think about this in bed before getting up for work. Weak morning light skirts the edge of the curtain and hits the plaque, enough to light up the golden scrollwork on just one corner. She can read ANY embossed in all caps. Once the light illuminates her whole name, she finally gets up and turns on the coffee pot.

In the back corner of the shower is a splotch of mold that's steadily creeping up the wall. It's stained the tiles a dank black and she calls it the Holy Ghost on mornings when she's feeling funny. The splotch has doubled in size over the past few weeks, because she just doesn't care enough to bleach it. Bethany collects bottles of bubble bath and body wash and different kinds of shampoo and conditioner, and water puddles under those bottles and makes the mold situation even worse. She buys shampoo made from organic ingredients that sound healthy, or maybe she'd seen it in an ad promoted by a woman whose hair looked especially thick, or body wash made from the extracts of rare plants because if it makes the plant special, shouldn't it work for her hair? She'd picked up this habit from her mother. Both Dolan women liked buying stuff, but her mother mostly bought bath salts. One of Bethany's earliest memories is watching her mother float in the milky blue and purple water, her skin hued like mermaid scales, her hair a dark veil cloaking her thin shoulders and breasts.

Today Bethany chooses a shampoo made from green tea and mint. It's supposed to be soothing, but also invigorating; what the commercial called "hair-apy." When she'd seen it on late night TV, the slick-haired models had huffed scent from the bottles with their eyes closed. Stress lines and crow's feet were magically erased until their faces transformed into identical poreless masks. The women were transported from their bathrooms to a lush tropical paradise, complete with warbling birds and breeze-ruffled palms. Bethany wonders how it would feel to achieve that level of relaxation. She scrapes her nails against her scalp until the gentle tingling sensation gives way to a powerful burn.

As she rinses the soap from her hair, she runs a hand down her torso and feels for the thing that she's avoiding and simultaneously rubbing like a genie's magic lamp. There it sits, the lump lodged under the skin like a closed fist in her guts. Her hands, slick with bath wash, rub at her stomach in smaller, tighter circles, until the lump is shifting beneath her fingers. Bethany sometimes worries that if she presses too hard on the lump that it might disintegrate. This bothers her for two reasons: because that means whatever's stored inside the lump will swim into the rest of her body, a sprawling infection contaminating everything it touches, or the second reason, which worries her more— that then lump will be gone forever.

But today Bethany's lump is still there, a dependable presence wedged along the right-hand side of her bellybutton. She sucks in her breath and probes through the skin and muscle. The lump is about the size of a tangerine. When she'd discovered it last month, it had felt relatively smooth. It didn't hurt to touch, but she could feel the swelling in her abdomen, rocking beneath her belly when she moved. There was a tugging sensation, like what she'd always called a food baby after too many carbs. Her muscles stretched awkwardly around the foreign object as if waiting for a bowel movement.

There's a difference getting dressed post-bump. Not anything that people could see; at least not through her clothes. It's as if she's grown a new limb. Like a baby who's found her toes for the first time, she can't stop touching it just to make sure it's really there. When she buttons her pants, they're ill-fitting, even though she hasn't gained any weight. There's something blocking the smooth line of her stomach. Bethany's always liked beer and cake and ordering herself a cheese pizza on Friday nights, so it's not as if her stomach were hard and flat before the lump, but now it's noticeable.

For her office job, she wears cute smocked dresses or sweaters and loose-fit skirts with boots to offset the fact that her stomach feels full of marbles. She feels like waddling instead of walking, hunching in on herself as she paces to the front desk for her mail, or feeling strangely vulnerable when she bends to retrieve fallen objects off the floor. She'd crouched to grab a loose file folder next to her desk and it felt like everyone could see under her clothes. Her skin feels hypersensitive and tender. Even the elastic of her underwear bothers her, so she's stopped wearing any.

On the drive to work, Bethany turns on the radio. She doesn't listen to anything in particular, but she hates all of the morning talk radio. The voices are jarring and abrasive, designed to wake people up. Instead she surfs and always catches the last few notes of songs, so she never learns any of the lyrics. There's been one CD in her car for the last year and she keeps forgetting to put in a new one. The thought of listening to it again is exhausting, like a little sister who won't shut up that you just want out of your room. Or what she imagines that would feel like. Bethany's an only child.

At work, she puts on fresh coffee while her computer boots up, pouring out the old stuff that's swimming with grounds. It looks light, as if someone's run the water through the coffee filter twice. While the new pot drips, she cleans out her mug in the sink as the water tries to decide between lukewarm and cold. The brown stain inside her mug won't come out. She's worked at this job for six years and she's still not totally sure what to tell people when they ask what she does for a living. Everything's just data entry these days.

Her mother calls in the afternoon. Bethany talks with the phone held between her cheek and shoulder while she eats a Greek yogurt at her desk. The flavor's so tart that her mouth involuntarily waters and she drools a spitty white line down the exact center of her dress. She scrubs at it with her fingers and feels for the lump while her mother asks her about dinner plans next weekend.

"Do you want the chicken?"

"What chicken?"

"The one, the cheesy one." Her mother speaks like this all the time, like Bethany's in her brain too, and can understand what she's talking about without context.

"Whatever you think would be good. It's your birthday."

Most people wouldn't want to prepare their own birthday dinner, but Bethany can't cook and her mother won't eat at restaurants. The last time they'd gone out for food was when Bethany was still in middle school. They'd met her father there for a congratulatory dinner on a recent job promotion. It was an Italian restaurant with paper tablecloths you could draw on with red and green waxy crayons, the cheap kind, and the bread was heavily coated with yellow garlic butter that smeared into Bethany's hair when she leaned over the plate. It was a Friday night and their waitress had bustled back and forth between tables and never refilled their water glasses. Her mother had sat there with her empty glass dangling from her hand, muttering: *I wish I had some water to drink right now* and *you know what would really hit the spot? Some ice water, that sounds refreshing* and *God, I am just so parched.* When it had come time to pay the check, her mother hadn't wanted them to give a tip. Bethany had seen her father try and slip a five under his plate, and her mother had seen it, too, and then she'd bit into her lip until the skin turned white.

"I don't know. I think maybe the chicken."

"That's fine." Bethany licks her finger and rubs at the yogurt stain on her dress. "What should I bring?"

"Maybe some rolls. No. A bag of ice."

Bethany's mother won't use the ice maker on the fridge. She says it tastes like chlorine.

"Okay. I'll pick up some chardonnay."

Her mother's going to be forty-nine which makes Bethany thirty-three. Sometimes people mistake the two of them for sisters, and Bethany's mother laughs until the smile lines dimple her cheeks. She tells Bethany maybe she should grow her hair out a little longer if she wants to appreciate her thirties and not skip straight over to fifty.

The lump to the right of Bethany's bellybutton is five weeks old. That's older than most of Bethany's relationships.

At two in the afternoon, she meets her friend Molly for lunch at the park midway between their jobs. Molly works as a bank teller. She always walks to the park in sneakers she keeps in her desk drawer, but Bethany drives her car and parks in the lot. She'd tried walking a few times, but the humidity makes her skin feel coated with a fine layer of cooking grease. Even though they've only been outside for ten minutes, Bethany can already feel it happening. She dabs at her forehead with the corner of a paper napkin and it comes back stained. She'd snagged a stack of them from the McDonald's when she'd picked up a couple of dollar chicken sandwiches and a medium vanilla shake. Molly's having a salad that smells like balsamic vinegar when she opens her Tupperware.

"What's with this? Two?" Molly points her fork at Bethany's lunch. There's a sliver of apple wedged between the tines.

"I'll probably have a light dinner."

As she'd sat in the drive thru, Bethany had felt the lump nestled beneath her seatbelt and ordered the extra sandwich. Even now, as she chewed her food, she thought that maybe she should start eating healthier. Most days she either picked up frozen meals or made pasta with a cheap bottle of red wine and then drank the rest of it while she watched late night television.

"So what's going on this weekend, you got a date with Kirya?"

"Date with my Mom."

There's too much mayonnaise on her chicken sandwich. Bethany peels open the bun and wipes it down with a napkin. Some of the lettuce and mayo falls onto the grass by her knees.

"So bring her with you."

"That's hilarious."

"I'm not trying to be funny." Molly shoves in a big bite. A piece of carrot falls from her mouth while she talks. "There's no nice way to eat a salad, is there?"

Bethany focuses on chewing her sandwich and drinking her shake. It's liquefied in the twenty minutes since she'd bought it and now it tastes like warm milk. Bethany wonders how much calcium she's getting a day since she mostly eats cereal and ice cream. Sometimes she imagines kidney stones or calcium deposits because of her diet, but she's never cared enough to do anything about it. The lump pouches over the belt that cinches the waist of her dress. It feels heavy. When she prods at it, there's a squirrely sensation below her belly button, as if there were fingers scrabbling at the underside of her skin.

Molly takes another bite of salad. "Indigestion from your super healthy lunch?"

"I probably need some Rolaids." Bethany pulls up her knees and stretches her arms over her head. It feels like the lump in her gut is doing somersaults off of nearby internal organs.

Alone in her car, she leans the seat all the way back. The air conditioning runs full blast as she tries to calm down. There's an overly full feeling that won't leave her alone, as if her stomach is complaining about what she'd decided to eat, but it wasn't really her stomach. It was more like the lump had needs, and Bethany was doing a shitty job accommodating them.

The radio played soft top forty and a song came on she recognized, one that she could remember Marjorie singing in her terrible, raspy voice, and it made Bethany's eyes tear up. She turned it off and listened to her stomach percolating. There was also the sound of the wind buffeting the car on either side as it whipped through the tops of the trees like fingers ruffling hair. White ibis huddled near the center of the park, flocking in tandem as they moved from one grassy patch to another. Bethany couldn't hear the noises they made, but she imagined scuffling and squawking.

She called in sick to work and went home to her couch.

Bethany had always wished for a twin. Not a sister or sibling, not anyone to take the spotlight from her already busy mother and father, but someone indistinguishable from her. Someone who'd share everything and take nothing, a person to tell intimate secrets, share birthdays and the same face, someone who'd understand Bethany without having to express things out loud. The longing had been so complex that she'd fantasized about her own twin, one she'd named Tabitha Dolan. This hadn't been an imaginary friend. She'd never been able to fully flesh out the body of this person, or let herself pretend she was real, but when she'd been in elementary school and needing someone, she'd looked into the mirror and seen her own face and had conversations with herself. She'd watched the way her lips shaped sounds, how her jaw would flex and relax, and stare at the crowded teeth gathered at the front of her mouth. As she'd gotten older, she'd let it go, but even now she found twinship fascinating. She pored over stories of twins separated at birth. These people had never met, but still led remarkably similar lives. Two women from Albuquerque had lived within fifteen miles of each other. Both of them had been schoolteachers, had appendectomies, and borne two daughters and had sons who'd died in infancy. Both women had married men named Robert.

Then there'd been the other twins. Conjoined by the legs, hands, heads, and torsos. Women with two arms or four, doppelgangers sharing stomachs, spines, and intestines. Their profiles were perfect mirrors. Twins with constant access to their doubles. They didn't necessarily need or want outside intimacy, but sometimes did, and they married or divorced indiscriminately. It wasn't the bodies that Bethany coveted. It was that there was someone who couldn't separate from you without dying; that you couldn't tell where you ended or where the other person began. The stories made Bethany's heart pound until she could nearly feel the double rhythm of her own phantom twin.

Though Bethany means "house of dates," Tabitha was the name of a woman raised from the dead by Saint Peter. She pats the lump in her belly and thinks about this some more. There are three syllables, like her name, with emphasis falling on the sounds that give them significance—the buh of the b and the voiceless dental fricative of the soft th that swallows the tongue near the end. There was a plaque she'd bought in middle school from a hallmark store in the mall, one that scribed the meaning of Tabitha in gilt, one that looked a lot like her own plaque. She'd kept it on the nightstand in middle school.

Her mother had asked why she'd bought it, and Bethany had said she'd maybe name her daughter that one day and it could be a keepsake. Now she wonders if she still has the plaque—it might be jammed into one of the boxes under her bed?

She pulls the cord for the light in the ceiling fan and then sits on the floor in her t-shirt and underwear. The braided rug cuts into the skin of her bottom while she reaches beneath the mattress to dig out the long blue Tupperware containers where she still keeps a lot of her old stuff. All her home memories from before she moved out with her first girlfriend, Marjorie. A woman she'd told her mother was her classmate, a college friend. They'd never had any classes together because they didn't actually go to the same school, because Bethany went to the junior college and Marjorie was taking classes at the tech school. When her mother would visit every Sunday afternoon, Marjorie would leave the apartment. Bethany would sit with her mother in the living room she'd scoured of all their personal pictures. They ate lunch together at the small kitchen table and pretended that the guestroom that Bethany said was her room wasn't just a catchall for their superfluous junk.

This is the apartment where Bethany still lives. After four years of faking commitment, Marjorie had moved out and taken half her stuff with her. Then there was Amber for a year, with all of her Pentecostal baggage—which Bethany had thought would bring them closer, but had made her self-loathing even worse. Isis came next. That lasted six months. She was significantly younger than Bethany and experimenting. When Isis had moved out, her new boyfriend loaded her stuff into a brand new pickup the color of a school bus. Bethany had helped him cart all of the things down to the curb while Isis sat in the cab with her face jammed into her phone. Bethany has lived alone ever since.

The plaque isn't in the Tupperware boxes, but there are framed photographs and her journals and an old address book from high school. She wonders if anyone would pick up if she called the phone numbers. Bethany lies back on the floor and drags her shirt up until her belly skin gets chilled from the ceiling fan. The lump is firm, and almost feels ridged. When she presses her fingers flat against the top of it, she's holding hands with the lump. It's part of her, and it feels feminine. She tries out the name, just to see what it might taste like in her mouth:

"Tabitha," she says. "Tabby Cat."

The lump in her guts shifts when she presses deep with her fingers. From her spot on the floor, she can see that she needs to vacuum. There's a lot of old dust and lint from places where her sweaters have shed all over the rug, and there's downy-white cat hair. There hasn't been a cat in the apartment since Isis left, and that was three years ago. Kirya hasn't come over yet, but Bethany's been thinking about it. She wonders if someone else's hands on her naked body will be able to feel the lump. The idea makes her nervous. She thinks she'll wait awhile before asking anyone over for dinner.

Ice melts in the front seat of Bethany's car. She's pulling into the neighborhood where she grew up with both her parents, but when she parks in the driveway, there's only her mother's brown sedan. There's a lot of pollen this time of year, and the car looks chalked, as if someone's clapped erasers nearby. Bethany knows her father's car is in the garage, trapped under a dark blue tarp, because she's the one who covered it when her mother couldn't stand to look at it any more.

She unlocks the front door with a key she keeps on her keychain. There's one for her car, one for her apartment, one for her mother's house, and one for Marjorie's old green Subaru. She can't let that one go. When she takes it off her keychain, her hand hovers over the garbage can, but she always puts it back in the bowl next to the front door. Then after too much wine with dinner, it winds up back on her key ring.

"You picked up rolls?"

"And the ice and the wine."

The television is on in the living room. It's muted, but Bethany knows what they're talking about. Her mother's watching reruns of *The Brady Bunch* again. Marsha's got her head tilted and her sleepy eyes focused on her two younger sisters. She's talking about something important, but Bethany doesn't watch Marsha. She looks at Jan. When she watched these episodes originally, she'd felt such crushing love that she'd found herself sketching Bethany Brady on her school folders, doodling hearts around the name. Her mother thought it was about Greg Brady, so she'd bought her a gigantic poster for her birthday of Greg holding a guitar, smiling hugely, wearing wide-legged brown pants. Bethany had taped it over her headboard. At night when she came back from the bathroom, stumbling around, half-asleep, she startled, afraid a strange man had come into her room. When she talked about the show at school, people thought she was weird. No one else watched those reruns.

In the kitchen, her mother slices lemon at the countertop. There are already vegetables grouped in small piles—the purple onions butted up against the white, green bell peppers cubed and dropped into the center of yellow and red, mushrooms carved into fours so that they look like arrow tips. There's spinach bunched up in the sink, which means Bethany will need to blanch it and also get out the black pepper. Her mother doesn't even like spinach.

First she puts the ice in the freezer. It's half-melted, which means it will harden into a block of something she'll probably need to chip at with an ice pick. Then she kisses the back of her mother's neck. It's bare except for wisps of black and gray from where it's pulled up into a high ponytail. Her mother's neck is very arched, with a strong jawline that still manages to look delicate. Bethany's own jaw is recessed like her father's. Sometimes she wonders if she makes decisions purely based on her bone structure. If she'd been born with a stronger jaw, maybe her backbone would have followed suit.

"Happy birthday, Mom."

"Could you finish these? I need to check the rice."

There's half a lemon left. The slices sit on the wooden block like opaque smiles, gap-toothed with seeds. Bethany waits until her mother's moved over to the stovetop to begin slicing. Her mother has very specific ways she likes to do things. Veggies in cubes, citrus wafered into thin fans, and asparagus cleaned in the sink and lopped at the end, like docking a dog's tail. Bethany doesn't spend time in her own kitchen. There are still spices leftover from Marjorie, who'd liked to bake. Now Bethany can't even enjoy pie without thinking about the time the oven caught on fire. They'd had to air out the house with all the windows open in summer, lounging around in just t-shirts and underwear.

Steam boils from the open mouth of the pot. Her mother scrapes the rice with a fork to get the stuff that's stuck to the very bottom, because one side of the coil always heats a little hotter than the other. Her father had always liked those crispy bits the best. The noise the fork makes as it scrapes against the metal makes Bethany want to throw the lemons. Instead she sticks one of her fingers in her mouth to bite at her nail and comes away with a tongue full of bitter pulp. The lump in her stomach quivers, flipping like a fish in a small bowl. She presses her hand to her stomach and lets her fingers settle in the ridges. She measures it with her hand, leaning back to look at her stomach, to see if she can make out the shape beneath her dress. Sometimes she thinks it's getting bigger, but it's not. The lump is always just large enough to fit in the cup of her palm.

"Too thick," her mother says. "Let me do it."

Bethany sits down at the kitchen table and plays with a pen she finds on a stack of bills, clicking and unclicking, while her mother moves back and forth between the piles of food, constructing miniature pyramids.

"How are you feeling?" Her mother asks this with her back turned, scooping up the diced onions and transferring them to the pot of rice without dropping anything.

"Okay. Fine." Bethany's phone rings. It's Kirya calling about dinner next week. She puts it on silent and zippers it into the front pocket of her purse when her mother gives her a strange look.

"Who was that?"

"Nobody. Just work."

Ink glops onto an open bill. Bethany smears it with her finger. She writes Tabby and Tabitha and Tab with her nail, staining it blue. When she sticks her finger back in her mouth, it tastes medicinal and still sour from the lemon juice. She wonders if she should start taking vitamins. She stands up and gets the plates out of the cabinet to set the table.

The dining table is just off the living room. Bethany wants to turn up the volume of the television because this is the episode where Jan has to get glasses and crashes her bike, but she knows that her mother can't stand to have the TV on while they're eating. Her mother carries in the dish of chicken with potholders covering each hand. Bethany sets the table, the lump in her stomach swinging down every time she leans over to put out the silverware. She grabs paper towels from the rack, but her mother brings out cloth napkins, so Bethany folds them on her lap and tells herself she'll use them later when she cleans the dishes.

As they eat, her mother pours wine from the large bottle that sits to the right of her dinner plate. There's crushed ice in the glass, because Bethany's mother is the kind of woman who puts ice in her white wine. Normally she'd say something about this, but it's her mother's birthday, so she'll leave it alone. She's brought her mother a gift, but she's forgotten it in the backseat of the car. It's candied blood orange body scrub and it's wrapped in blue and white paisley tissue paper. Bethany wonders if sitting out in the heat will ruin the soap.

"Can I pour you some?" Her mother's already tipping the bottle over.

"No, just the water."

"Are you sure? It's pretty good." Her mother's still pouring, though it's slowed to a trickle that leaks down the side of the glass.

"Just water."

Bethany forks a stack of lemon slices, dumping five of them in her water. They float on top of the ice and turn the water cloudy. There's another glass set out at the other end of the table, even though Bethany didn't put it there. An empty plate with silverware lined up at either side; things that'll just be put away again without needing to be washed.

Bethany digs into her bread and smears cheese from the chicken into the middle. "So what did you do today? Did you get any good cards?"

Her mother volunteers at the church preschool two days a week and the kids are always giving her things—drawings, sculptures made from bits of dough, small plastic figurines and beaded necklaces. Bethany's mother keeps everything on display in her bedroom.

"A few things." Her mother chews her chicken and then finishes her glass of wine before pouring another. The ice crackles from the heat of the wine. "I went to visit your father."

"You mean you went to the cemetery."

Wine slops onto the tablecloth. There's a big wet ring around her mother's glass. "Why do you have to say it like that?"

"Like what?"

"Like it's the equivalent of pumping gas."

"Because it makes me sad." Bethany reaches over and mops up the spill with the paper towels from her lap.

"Why?" Her mother takes another sip of wine. "Because I chose to spend my birthday with my husband?"

"No, because you keep talking about him like he's still here."

"That's offensive, Bethany."

"I'm sorry."

The conflict hurts Bethany's stomach. She drinks more water to help disperse the acid building behind the lump, but the lemon makes it worse. She eats more of the bread and then helps herself to some of the pitted black olives that her mother's piled into a little serving dish. There is a shiny pile of them heaped next to green baby pickles and the red and yellow peppers.

"What are you doing?"

"Eating." The olives are salty and delicious. She grabs more of them and sticks two in her mouth at once.

"You hate olives," her mother says. "You haven't eaten an olive since the fourth grade when you threw them up all over your Easter dress."

Bethany stops chewing and lets the flavor sit on her tongue. It's oily and bitter. "I guess I like them now."

"I know what you're doing." Her mother stares at her while the lump in Bethany's stomach twists into itself. "I know what this is."

She thinks about the call from Kirya. She wonders how she'll explain this in a way that's not going to make her sick.

"It's a baby. You're pregnant." Her mother's crying. "The olives, just like me."

Bethany clutches her stomach. The lump sits off to one side, heavy, pouching over the elastic of her underwear. She opens her mouth, but doesn't know how she can explain this new part of her anatomy that's obviously not a baby. Her mother gets up from her seat and kneels beside Bethany's chair, putting both hands over Bethany's, gently pressing over the lump.

"This is so wonderful." Her mother's breath smells sour, like the wine she's been drinking. "A baby."

Olives have rolled to either corner of Bethany's plate. She's staring at them while her mother pats her belly like there's new life inside, ready to kick, and that's when her stomach growls. Her mother laughs and hugs her, and the lump presses between both of their bodies. Bethany rubs her mother's back, and she's still clutching the paper towels, soaking wine into her mother's new birthday shirt.

There's a bottle of kid's two-in-one in the shower, unopened. She bought it because it was shaped like a tropical fish and it smelled like a grape-scented marker. Now she uses it to scrub at her hair, which is thinning and flat, no matter what combination of shampoos she's tried. The smell is overwhelming, like huffing powdered drink mix. She keeps washing herself with it, lathering and re-lathering her body, her face, and her frizzy pubic hair.

Mostly she rubs over the lump. It's not a baby, but it feels like something alive and part of her. When her mother had pressed her hands over top of it, she'd felt scared. As if her mother's happiness could infect the thing inside her and turn it into a medical problem, not the wishful thinking that she'd been putting on it for the past few weeks. It became something that wouldn't magically disappear overnight; it would expand and take over her life.

On the drive home, she'd picked up another bottle of wine. Then she'd called Kirya and the two of them had sat on the couch, watching television. They'd drank that bottle of wine and then they'd finished another she'd found stashed at the back of her fridge. Later, when they were rolling around in bed together, Bethany could feel the lump between them. It was like a fist gripping the muscles of her abdomen. She'd wondered if Kirya could feel it too, lumped beneath the skin of her stomach, a swollen mass alongside a bulging stomach of carbs and wine.

Now she's showering while Kirya waits for her in the bedroom, soaping herself again and again. The water's turned icy and it's slicing sharply against her shoulders, until she's so cold that her skin feels shrunken, too tight to fit over her bones. In the mirror, her reflection is pale and drained. Spots darken her skin, reminders of past blemishes that still haven't healed and etched grooves set around her eyes. There's an unfamiliar sallowness to her skin, something radiating ill health.

In the bedroom, Bethany walks to the bed and drops her towel. She takes both Kirya's hands and presses them to her stomach. The lump squirms, moving awkwardly beneath the skin as Bethany sucks in air to try and make the bump more pronounced.

"What are you doing?" Kirya wiggles her fingers and the mass quivers beneath her touch.

"Do you feel it?" Bethany asks.

Kirya shakes her head, so Bethany presses harder. Kirya's hands are warm, but her touch is insubstantial. No matter how hard Bethany presses, the lump is the only body anchoring her to reality. It's the only solid force in the universe.

Kirya kisses her stomach. "You smell good," she says. "Like baby medicine."

Bethany climbs back into the bed. She lets Kirya roll on top of her and tries to will the lump through their bodies, so they can attach themselves to each other. The lump resists. It sits hard and heavy beside her bellybutton, pulling at her organs.

Felt in the Jaw

Tammy thought her backyard never looked so much like a vacant lot as it did at twilight. The grass stood tall and weedy in some parts alongside bare patches of dirt where the ground was scraped and dead. Anthills poked up at odd intervals, the ants threading back and forth between them in red and black highways. At dusk the sun sat like a fat Easter egg, its dye running burnt orange through the branches of the trees.

"Out of the way." Tammy pointed at her oldest with the end of a tent pole. "Get your sister a marshmallow."

The air was thick with humidity and the smell of damp leaves, which probably meant rain. It wasn't ideal weather for an outdoor birthday party for her youngest daughter, but it was too late for a change of plans. There was no cake and streamers, just Tammy and her two girls camped out under the stars.

"Can we split a candy bar?" Laura waggled the bag of minis in her face.

"No," Tammy said, then ignored when her daughters opened the bag anyway.

They were using the red pup tent she'd gotten her youngest as a birthday gift. It had cost less than thirty dollars, which was good because her budget was already stretched thin. There'd been few present options that didn't seem cheap or meaningless, so when she'd finally found the tent sitting alone on the shelf, it had felt like kismet. She'd stood in the store aisle, holding the box, dreaming up memories with her daughters that would last a lifetime—gathering wood from their yard for a campfire, crunching on trail mix in ziplock bags, breathing in the cool night air and drifting peacefully off to sleep. She'd picked up a few dollar flashlights and a tiny Igloo cooler for sodas and figured she'd assemble the tent around noon, which would give them plenty of time for activities.

It took three hours to set up. Tammy wormed the rods through the small plastic openings as the grass and weeds itched her ankles. The bugs flew directly at her face no matter how hard she swatted at them, attracted by the sweat beading above her lip and along her hairline. There were mosquito larvae wriggling in the puddle water out back by the shed, their bodies rolling in the plant detritus and muck. By the number of bites dotting her arms and legs, Tammy imagined she'd have malaria by the end of the night. But her daughter's face had lit up with excitement once the tent finally stood upright on its shaky legs, and the torture had seemed worthwhile.

Sitting inside its warm red glow felt like curling up in a cozy cabin. Tammy wanted to read the girls from the *Little House* books, but they rolled their eyes at her. Instead they'd wanted to tell each other scary stories with the flashlight pressed under their chins, their missing baby teeth turning their faces into hollowed out jack-o-lanterns.

Tammy didn't think this was such a great idea. Laura was her oldest and she loved to scare her younger sister—she was smart and loud and quick to get angry when people told her no. Maggie was her youngest and her sweetheart, though she cried easily and hated doing anything that might make her sweaty. She was already complaining about the dirt on her shorts after the first fifteen minutes of sitting outside, and Tammy was beginning to feel sorry she'd planned something as "simple" as a backyard campout.

But there'd been s'mores, and though they'd been messy, they'd been delicious and the girls had each had four. She'd been able to coax fire from the damp wood with the help of some strangled bits of newspaper, crunched up in her kids' sweaty palms. They'd eaten hotdogs cooked on bent coat hangers and they'd tasted okay and the kids had actually eaten them. The fire had a comfortable smell that made Tammy feel happy, like bundling up under blankets. Even the choking, smoky parts fed her nostrils like Christmastime, reminding her of cold nights when her father had played the guitar for their family and they'd sat around the fireplace and eaten popcorn balls. She and her girls sang silly songs, commercial jingles and patriotic anthems, and when they'd gotten tired out they'd all crawled inside the tent together. It was just as cozy as she'd imagined; the three sleeping bags piled nearly on top of each other, her two babies snuggled on either side of her. For the first time since her wife had left, they'd felt like a family again. Tammy was able to smile and mean it for a few minutes before she'd drifted off in the sweltering plastic of the tent.

When the bite happened, Tammy hadn't even opened her eyes. She'd stayed in the barely cognizant place between wake and sleep, rubbing at the spot with one hand twisted up behind her back in the sleeping bag. It had felt like the start of an ingrown hair or maybe a pimple. The pain was sharp and sudden, but not anything worth waking the kids over. Tammy decided to ignore it, burrowing down, pulling the sleeping bag over her face and dropping right back to sleep.

Tammy woke again abruptly sometime later, her stomach roiling. She sat up and pressed a hand against her back, which ached, as if she'd slept with her spine curled around a metal pole. It was dark in the tent, but she could feel Maggie's leg, kicked out from her sleeping bag, which made Tammy think she'd received an accidental kick to the kidney. Then her stomach pitched again, and she wondered if it would help to use the bathroom or if she could even try to do that without waking up either one of the girls. Maybe she'd had too many hot dogs—or maybe they'd gone bad? She'd bought the grocery store brand because they were cheaper. She hoped her kids wouldn't get sick.

Her stomach lurched and she scrambled to sit up. Tammy fumbled for her flashlight, fingertips skimming the slippery tops of sleeping bags and grazing the soft skin of an arm. After digging between the pillows, she finally found her phone. She brought it up to her face and clicked one of the buttons. The blue glow made her eyes want to seal shut again.

"Momma?"

"Go back to sleep, baby, it's fine." She pushed her youngest daughter's head back down against her pillow. Maggie's hair was drenched with sweat.

The screen on her phone told her that it was after two in the morning. There was a heavy feeling in her bladder and a sharp pain behind her eyes. Tammy worked the sleeping bag down her legs and immediately started shivering. Her fingers trembled and the phone screen shook in her hand. There were two emails from work that she ignored and a curt text from her ex about when she'd be by the next day to pick up the kids. She put down the phone and crawled to the front of the tent, sliding her knees slowly along the ground so she wouldn't pull anyone's hair or smash any fingers. The tent's front was zippered closed and she fumbled for the tab. When she found it, the zipper stuck in three places before finally opening a hole wide enough for her to crawl through into a drizzle. As she peeled apart the tent flaps and pushed her head through the gap, drips fell into her hair. Her teeth chattered violently.

Overhead the moon was a pale smudge behind the low-hanging clouds. She wasn't wearing shoes and she hadn't mown the grass in a few weeks, so the weeds slapped wetly against her legs. Tiny moths and other bugs floated up from the ground, drifting past her face as she made her way to the house. Melissa always used to mow the lawn, that was her thing, and Tammy had taken out the garbage and cleaned the bathrooms. Now Tammy had to do all those things and work full time and plan a camping trip in the backyard with half of the money it took to do it. Everything felt too hard all the time, like trying to do three people's jobs, which left her irritable and exhausted. Tammy wasn't sure how she'd get anything done if she was actually sick.

The sliding door looked like the entrance to a cave. She flattened her hands against the glass and felt her back twinge sharply, as if someone had grabbed a fistful of her muscles. She'd left the air conditioning running in the house, and the cold combined with the humidity outside dragged up a layer of goosebumps on her skin. Her teeth began to chatter again, and she couldn't get them to stop even when she grit them together. The living room was dark, but she knew her way around even without the light to guide her. They'd owned the house for seven years, and even though Melissa wanted to sell it, Tammy had outright refused. She'd shaped the way the furniture sat, picked the rug for the front hall, and brought her babies home to their freshly painted rooms. Their childhood artwork cluttered its walls and their growth was marked on the wall next to the garage.

Her eyes burned as she clicked on the wall switch in the hall bathroom and the buttery yellow halogens came on over the mirror. Tammy had avoided looking at her reflection for a while now. Her appearance was always shocking to her—the enlarged pores on her cheeks and nose, the stray dark hairs sprouting up under her chin— things that she hadn't noticed even six months ago. After Laura, her flesh had gone a little doughy, but after Maggie it had permanently dented and dimpled at her waist and hips. The creases in her neck looked like the trunk of a tree. As she leaned in, she saw that the whites of her eyes were flushed bright pink, and as she moved in closer to get a better look, the muscles in her back seized up. She fell against the sink, banging her hip against the edge of the vanity.

"Oh god, shit." The pain came in waves, cresting and falling before building up again to something unbearable. She reached her hand beneath her shirt and rubbed at her back. There was an ice pick feeling that ran down her spine as if someone had stabbed her. When she pulled up the hem of her t-shirt and twisted sideways, there was a mark in the center of her back. It was an angry red, streaked and dark, like someone had pressed a lit cigarette to her skin. She touched it gently with the tips of her fingers and blinked to clear the sleep from her eyes. She'd left her glasses in the bedroom, hadn't thought to bring them out into the tent where one of the girls could step on them in the middle of the night. It hurt to touch the mark; it was radiating heat and looked puffy.

There was ibuprofen in the medicine cabinet. The bottle rattled loudly. Only three pills left. She thought about the grocery list she always kept on the fridge and how there was no one left to go to the store. Melissa used to pick up groceries and Tammy had written the list. Tammy had loaded the dishwasher and Melissa had unloaded it. One of them would take the garbage cans out to the curb for pick up on Monday evenings, and the other would drag the empty cans back up to the house the following afternoon. Tammy missed their easy routines almost as much as she missed having a body beside her in bed every night. There were other medicines up in the cabinet, leftover prescription bottles that weren't hers that were probably expired. Melissa used to make her keep everything, old leftover oxycodone from a root canal, hydrocodone from a pretty miserable ear infection four years ago. When she'd tried to throw them out, Melissa had been livid.

What if one of us gets hurt? Melissa had dug the orange plastic bottles out of the trash and wiped the coffee grounds from their sides.

Then we'd go to the doctor. Tammy thought that was self-explanatory.

What if we couldn't afford it? Melissa had asked. The prescription had been old already; the typescript on the label had begun to fade. *What would we do then?*

Tammy looked at those bottles now and understood. She set them both on the counter, just in case the ibuprofen wasn't enough. She swallowed down the three pills with a handful of water from the tap, and when she bent over to drink from her palm, the slicing pain up her back almost made her choke on them.

She walked back through the darkened house. Colors swam in her eyes, so she stopped behind the couch and pressed her hands down into the cushion while she tried to reorient herself. Her phone was still in the tent with the girls. She wondered if she'd have to call for an ambulance or if she'd be able to drive herself. How did a person know it was time to call the hospital? Didn't someone else usually make those decisions? Her insurance hadn't kicked in yet at her job, the new overpriced plan she'd had to take since she couldn't be on Melissa's insurance anymore. How much would an overnight visit be out-of-pocket?

Tammy pressed her face against the sliding glass door to look outside and let the coolness soothe her. When she lifted her forehead, she saw she'd left a rectangular smear of grease. Her hair was dirty and tangled. When she brushed it off her face and neck, her skin felt like boiled chicken.

"I need a shower," she said. "I can't go anywhere like this."

Instead of bathing, she walked back out into the yard. She was unsteady, leaning forward, hoping that would help her back not hurt as much. There was a large branch that had fallen after a thunderstorm the previous week, and bits of broken stick jabbed her bare feet. When she reached the orange tree in the center of the yard, her stomach protested and she leaned against the trunk and threw up. What came out was a mix of hot dogs and barely digested pills, which were chalky and bitter. The taste of it made her gag again, so she wiped her tongue on the hem of her t-shirt. She stayed bent in half for a second, panting, worried what would happen when she tried to stand up again.

"Mom?" Laura poked her head through the flaps of the tent. "What's wrong?"

"Nothing, go back to sleep."

"Are you sick?"

Tammy's oldest was a noted hypochondriac. If someone complained of a sore throat, suddenly Laura had the flu. When Maggie had broken one of her fingers in a slammed car door, Laura had worn a sling around for a week and claimed she'd broken her arm falling off the backyard tire swing.

"No, just trying to cool off. It's hot in the tent."

"I'm hot, too."

"I'm coming back inside," Tammy said. "Don't wake your sister."

Her girls needed her. There was nothing else she could do. Tammy stood up slowly, the muscles in her back spasming violently. Laura had found one of the flashlights and was shining it in Tammy's face, nearly blinding her.

"You don't look so good."

Tammy fought the urge to throw up again. "Move, please."

Laura backed up and Tammy got to her knees and crawled inside the tent. She opened up her sleeping bag to climb back in, and then thought better of it.

"Give me the flashlight."

Laura handed it to her and Tammy pointed it at the inside of her sleeping bag. At first all she saw was pilled up felt and a hole where the stuffing had started to pull loose in one of the corners. Then her eyes focused and she saw a dark blob near one of the middle seams of the sleeping bag. She brought the light closer and made out spindly legs and a black torso—the crushed body of a spider. She prodded it with the front lip of the flashlight to see if it was still alive, and the legs jerked. Tammy brought down the flashlight and crushed it. Laura leaned over her to see and Tammy snapped off the light, pitching them into darkness.

"What was it? A bug?"

"No, just a leaf that was poking me. Let's go to sleep now before you wake up Maggie."

"I'm awake." Maggie rolled over onto her side and put her hand on Tammy's leg. "I'm thirsty."

Tammy's teeth clenched and her jaw ached. Whenever she tried to relax her muscles, her teeth started chattering again. She used the side of her hand to swipe out the remnants of the spider and then climbed back into her sleeping bag, pulling it up to her chin.

"I'm hot, I want to go inside."

"Me too." Maggie's voice was near her ear. "Momma, I'm thirsty, though."

"Please go to sleep." Tammy pulled the sleeping bag up over her head. She couldn't handle dealing with the girls, not with how she was feeling. The last time she'd been really sick had been the time Maggie brought home the flu from pre-k, and they'd all come down with it. It had been miserable—throwing up in different bathrooms, the body aches, huddling together in their big bed and watching cartoons until Tammy wanted to scream at them all to get out and leave her alone, to let her be sick in peace. At the time she thought that nothing could be worse than that feeling.

One of the girls prodded at her back with their fingers, and she bit into the stuffing of the sleeping bag to keep from yelling.

"Momma, please. I'm thirsty."

"I said *go to sleep.*"

Tammy didn't use that voice very often, and it wasn't one she'd ever used on her daughters. She was the nice mom, the one who let the girls stay up late and eat cereal for dinner. This was the tone she once used on an unfriendly dog that had come up behind her when she was out jogging, pressing its teeth against her leg and growling. She was so scared that she'd used the deepest, worst voice she could think of to get the dog to leave her alone—a voice that said I am meaner than you think I am, and if you keep doing what you're doing I will hurt you.

Maggie rolled over and cried into her sleeping bag.

Tammy's teeth chattered and she pressed her hand up into her cheek to massage the growing ache. It was a burrowing pain, like she'd bitten down on something and her jaw had cracked. She hoped that there was still something left of the ibuprofen in her stomach from when she'd thrown up in the yard. Getting up to get more medicine seemed impossible. Tammy counted the seconds it took to breathe in and then breathe out over the space of five lungfuls of air. She repeated it until she finally fell back to sleep.

When she woke again, it was still dark in the tent. She'd been having a dream that she was at a chiropractor and he was digging his fingers deep into her back. She asked him to stop, but he just kept pushing, saying it always hurts at first, but then the hurt makes it feel better. She wanted to get up from the table but her legs were in stirrups, like how it was when she'd gone to the OB/GYN, or when she'd had her babies and her partner Melissa had hovered over her like a restless bird. When she cracked open her eyes there was nothing to see, just noises: rustling coming from the left side of the tent nearest to the fence, scraping and crunching in the dead leaves. A stick fell over in the fire pit she'd had with the girls and made a clang when it banged against the metal lip.

There was a wet patch by her face on her pillow, the pillow from the bed that she'd taken from the house. There was just the one pillow left on her side now, because Melissa had taken her two when she'd left. For the nine years they'd been together, Melissa had two pillows and Tammy had one, so that when they slept side by side their heads were always raised at two different angles. They'd never been able to sleep comfortably because of it.

The pillowcase was dirty. She hadn't washed her sheets in weeks. It was hard to remember to take care of things for herself without Melissa there to remind her. She always remembered things for the girls—their chewable multivitamins, brown bag lunches for school—but never remembered to give herself medicine, or make sure that she ate the right amount of vegetables, or even to bring a sweater with her in case she got cold. Tammy could remember her mother caring for her when she was young, but mostly she remembered Melissa putting her hands against her fevered cheeks. She could remember the way those cool hands felt when they smoothed along the hot column of her neck. Tammy wondered if anyone would ever touch her neck again in just the right way that made her feel okay with her body. The kind of touch that understood all the bumps and ridges and dips before they even touched the skin, the way that she could remember the hands on her now without physical contact.

Melissa was supposed to pick up the girls tomorrow in the early afternoon and the house was a wreck. She wasn't going to be able to clean it in a way that made it look like she was doing fine on her own. They'd been together so long that she didn't know how to be by herself anymore, didn't know how to react when she talked with people or had to do things like make dinner. Now everything was for three or for one, odd numbers that confused her after so many years of even amounts. But she also didn't know Melissa anymore, definitely not the person who'd taken so few things from the house when she'd left. No furniture, no mementoes, not anything they'd bought together. Just enough clothes to fit into a single bag, the kind of luggage you took for a carry-on for a flight that would bring you back in three or four days.

Drips of sweat pooled in her lower back and her skin itched. When she reached behind her to swipe at it, the muscles in her back clenched and her teeth came down hard enough to bite through her lip. The blood tasted sharp on her tongue. Tammy tried to imagine the pain in her back as a tangible object; one she could push through her body and out of her mouth, tried to make her muscles relax back to their normal shape.

She was used to visualizing pain. Melissa had gotten migraines every few months. Tammy would darken the room and put the lavender powder on the sheets, and pull out the cooling cloth for her forehead. Then Tammy would sit on the side of the bed and feel the downy-soft hair at Melissa's scalp, scratching at her like she would one of their cats. The month before she'd moved out, Melissa had cropped off nearly all of her hair. The soft maple sugar curls that had been Tammy's favorite thing, sweet ringlets like a doll's hair, shorn off into a buzz cut that had turned her partner into a stranger. In moments where she was honest with herself, Tammy had wondered whether Melissa was sick, if maybe she had some kind of cancer, and Tammy hadn't wanted to know about it. She'd hoped Melissa wouldn't tell her, because all she could think about was how hard it would be on her and the kids if they had to watch Melissa collapse inward while the rest of the family orbited her like a dying star.

The noise outside the tent kept pulling Tammy in and out of sleep. She closed her eyes and tried to focus on where the pain was coming from, radiating through her lower back, but also in her legs. The tightness of her cheek and jaw was terrible. She wondered if she should call someone. Her parents lived four hours away, and her brother and sister both lived out of state. Their friends had been *their friends* and that made things hard. She couldn't stomach their pity.

Tammy pressed the speed dial for Melissa and wondered what she would do if someone else answered the phone—a voice she didn't recognize, or worse, a voice that she might know. The phone rang and rang and then it went to voicemail. Not even Melissa in the message, just a robotic answering service telling her she could leave a callback number.

There was a little bit of drool leaking from the side of her lip from where she was clenching her teeth and she wiped it away. The phone glowed bright all of a sudden and she saw Melissa's face close to her own. It was a picture of her partner from a few years back, a side shot in the sunlight with the kids at an amusement park. It had been a last minute stopover on their trip back from the mountains, coming home from a vacation that hadn't gone well. The amusement park had been rundown and it was off season. There'd been an animal safari tour where they hadn't seen a single animal aside from some ratty looking squirrels, and the girls had ridden on swings with long rusted chains that squealed every time they'd shifted in their seats. When she'd taken the picture, Melissa had been holding up a drippy waffle cone for one of the girls to lick, and she'd been frowning as the chocolate dripped down into her sleeve. Tammy had thought the picture was cute because it showed how aggravated Melissa looked all the time, but now it just seemed like she looked really unhappy, and maybe Tammy could have looked at this picture before Melissa had left and known what would eventually happen.

"Hello?"

"What's wrong?"

And the voice was like calling home from far away. It reminded Tammy of being at camp during summers when she was young, how she'd missed her family and would call them to come and get her. Everyone sounded really tinny and unreachable. Melissa's voice was like hearing home from a very long distance and wondering if she'd ever get back there again.

"Is everything okay? Are the girls sick?"

"No." Tammy had to hold her breath so she wouldn't cry.

"Then what is it?"

Tammy listened to hear a second voice breathing in the background, a voice that might be in the bed with Melissa, maybe wrapping an arm around Melissa's middle, because even though Melissa was taller than everyone she knew, she always insisted on being the little spoon.

"Are you drunk?"

"No, I'm not drunk." Talking this much made her jaw ache. "Something happened."

"With the girls?"

"No, with me." Tammy could feel Melissa evaluating whether this was still her problem. "A spider. I think a spider bit me. It hurts."

"How do you know it was a spider?"

Tammy shifted and the muscles in her back creaked and groaned like an old mattress.

"There was a dead spider in the sleeping bag. It's a fucking spider bite, okay? Jesus Christ."

"Do you need to go to the hospital?"

"I don't know." Her whole body was on fire. When she rubbed her hand against her leg it came back sopping with sweat, like she'd been doused with a hose.

"I'll be over in a minute."

Melissa hung up in her ear. Tammy didn't know whether she felt relieved or disgusted with herself.

She must have fallen asleep again, because the next thing Tammy knew was that there was something touching her leg through the sleeping bag. It was aggravating, like being trapped by a seatbelt. When she kicked her leg to free herself, the muscles in her back clenched into one big cramp. She moaned low in her throat.

"Do you need me to come inside?" Melissa stuck her hand through the gap in the tent flaps.

"No," Tammy said. "I can do it."

She forced herself to sit up. Melissa's fingers wiggled at her as she crawled across the sleeping bag between her two daughters, their two daughters, and remembered so many things about those hands. How they'd touched her face and her thighs, how they were tough enough to open jars of spaghetti sauce, how they could play "Skylark" on the piano in their living room. Those hands had been in the delivery room, one holding Tammy's hand and the other one holding their firstborn baby, smiling down at her through watery eyes and a grin so big you'd have though Tammy had won an Olympic medal and not just pushed out a kid.

She let Melissa pull her up through the tent flaps and into the oppressive humidity. It was still dark, but Tammy could see that Melissa had driven over in her pajamas and that her hair had grown out into a softer, curlier cut than the last time they'd seen each other. Melissa helped her across the lawn and touched the small of her back, and it hurt Tammy to think that Melissa could still treat her so carefully, even though the last time they'd spoken over the phone the discussion had devolved into a screaming argument over whether the girls could stay with Melissa for an extra weekend next month.

Inside the house, they both walked straight to what had been their bathroom. Melissa dropped her hand and Tammy felt the disconnect like someone had carved them apart. Her own fingers trembled, so she clenched them into a fist.

"Did you take any of these?" Melissa held up one of the old prescription bottles.

"No, I took some ibuprofen, but I barfed them up."

"Do you know what kind of spider?"

"I don't know, it looked black, maybe?"

Tammy leaned against the counter and tried to take smaller breaths. Whenever she filled her lungs too full, she could feel them pressing against the muscles in her back, muscles stretched so tight that they felt rigid and breakable. The smell of Melissa was in the room too—like bread right out of the oven. When they'd first started dating, Tammy had called Melissa her Pillsbury dough boy and Melissa hadn't spoken to her for a week afterward.

"Is it okay we left the girls outside?" Tammy didn't want them to wake up and be afraid.

"Yeah, let them sleep." Melissa opened one of the prescription bottles and gave her one of the yellow pills. She filled up one of the little paper cups from the tap and handed it to Tammy.

"I don't think you need to go to the hospital, I think you just need sleep."

"I'm not sure." Tammy looked at the pill. "What if I get too sick?"

"I'll stay here. I'll sleep on the couch."

"You don't have to do that." Tammy thought about the possible warm body waiting back at Melissa's apartment, the probable friend that she knew, maybe a person of her acquaintance.

"It's fine, I'll stay."

"Don't you have someone waiting for you?" And she'd said it, but she couldn't look at Melissa's face to see her reaction.

"It doesn't matter."

The ache in Tammy's jaw intensified. It was sharp and pinching like all her feelings were being crushed between her back molars. She clenched her jaw and swallowed hard so she wouldn't cry in front of this person who owned nearly ten years of her life. Then Tammy opened her mouth and took the medicine. When she saw herself in the mirror over the sink, she couldn't reconcile what she saw with her own body—how her hair was greasy and dark, with white at the temples, like a dog that had suddenly aged without the owner's knowledge. Her lips were pale. She wondered how she was supposed to rework herself to promote what she had to a new person, like Melissa had done. How did people give everything of themselves to someone, their comfort, their sweetness and their horribleness, and then expect to give it to someone else all over again?

She leaned back against the counter. When her hip hit the granite, she cried out. Melissa grabbed her upper arms so she wouldn't fall over, and when she felt her hands on her skin, Tammy collapsed inward. She pressed her nose into the crook of Melissa's neck and inhaled. Melissa's hands were strong on her back and she felt something give, like a rubber band that's tensed to snap. Tammy's jaw unclenched, and it felt like it wanted to unhinge from itself like a snake and swallow Melissa whole.

Notice of a Fourth Location

When they asked, I said the woman looked like she was sleeping. She looked like I did every night in my living room, dozing beneath the flickering glow of the television set. The clear morning light lit her hair a deep blue-black and etched shadows on the apple of her cheek. It was a very sweet scene, and I felt weird looking at her through the van's back window, like I was spying on her in a private moment. That's exactly what I told the paramedics. For all we knew, she could have been napping on her couch.

Except the woman wasn't asleep. She was dead.

We were clumped around the beat up gray minivan in the middle of the shopping plaza parking lot. There were three of us still standing there, asking questions, not including the paramedics or the fireman. Only three of us, not including the dead woman, who was pulled from the van and hoisted neatly onto a stretcher not ten feet away from where we stood.

"Asphyxiation." The fireman was in his early twenties. His red face glistened with sweat, brown hair slicked flat against his round skull. The sun baked off the pavement in hot, wavy lines, but he still wore his rubbery fireman's coat. It smelled a little like a burnt tire. "It's extremely dangerous to stay in a car in this kind of heat—it's why it's against the law to leave your dog out here, even if you're only running into the store for a minute. It's never okay, but especially not June in Florida."

I nodded, though I already knew all this. It gave me something to do besides stare at the paramedics, who were taking vital signs in a slow, methodical way that implied the woman would never need them taken again.

"Did she kill herself?" Deanna was sixty-something in a pink velour tracksuit and bright white sneakers, the kind that looked like they'd been scrubbed clean with a toothbrush. She'd been the first to notice something was wrong with the woman, her scream as shrill as a scared child. A full grocery bag of produce was lumped on the asphalt next to her feet. The heat would likely bruise her apples.

"I'm not at liberty to say."

"You're not at liberty, or you just don't know?" Bob's hair was combed over in a way that showed wide stripes of scalp; it had flapped upright as we'd run across the parking lot, after Deanna had screamed and pointed at the van. Bob's cologne smelled like the kind sixteen-year-old kids wore, an aerosol spray assault on the body before it assaulted anyone's nose. "I bet you just don't know. Covering your bases, right?"

The fireman shrugged. "I'm not at liberty to say."

"Typical." Bob crossed his arms. He was holding an electric blue Gatorade that sweat fat drops onto the front of his navy blue suit jacket.

The woman lay dead under a sheet while the paramedics prepared the emergency vehicle. They loaded their gear slowly and talked to each other, the woman's body between them, on the stretcher, propped on the hot asphalt.

"This kind of thing happens more often than you'd think. Way too often." The fireman jerked his thumb at the minivan with its wide, untinted windows and its bald tires, as if the shitty car was the root of the problem, and not the sweltering heat that was burning the soles of my feet through my thin canvas shoes.

I hadn't thought I'd be out this long. I wasn't even wearing a bra under my t-shirt, and the shorts I was wearing were actually boxers I'd slept in the night before. Marissa had asked me to pick up some orange juice and the tubed cinnamon rolls she liked, the ones that came capped with a miniature tub of frosting. Ever since my wife had gotten pregnant, I was at her mercy when it came to mid-morning cravings. I was a web consultant and worked from home. It was the second time that week that I'd been in the parking lot.

"Will we need to provide a statement?" I asked. My eyes kept drifting to the sheet, then skipping over it and settling on the paramedics. Safer to glance at their faces. Easier to look at things that were moving like they should, muscles bunching and contracting, their arms moving in perfect unison as they put away their equipment.

"No, I don't think so. Maybe just you, ma'am." The firefighter motioned toward Deanna, who was looking down at her bags of groceries, still sitting clumped at her feet. She couldn't put them in her car. Too hot to keep the fruit from going bad. "The rest of you, we just need your contact information."

My phone vibrated in my pocket as I wrote my name in all caps across the top of the fireman's clipboard. The buzzing cut off, then started up again almost immediately. Marissa, wondering about her cinnamon rolls. Probably imagining me dead in a ditch somewhere, or being put onto a stretcher. Like the one that held the dead woman, who was casually hefted by the two attendants and put into the back of the ambulance.

"You all should move along. Go home or to work, wherever you're supposed to be." The firefighter wasn't looking at me or Bob when he said this; he was guiding Deanna over to a bench cloaked by the parking lot's solitary tree. I wasn't looking at him, either. I was staring at the ambulance as it pulled carefully onto the street, no lights or siren.

While I surfed the TV for breaking news, I explained everything to my wife. She sat with her swollen feet up on the couch, clutching our ginger tom, Samson, who was so overweight that he had recently developed sleep apnea.

"Oh my god," she said, convulsively stroking Samson's fat, furry back. "Oh my *god*."

"I know. It was awful."

Marissa closed her eyes and squeezed the cat to her chest, his fat belly perched on top of her own, five months full of baby. His strangled mewls gurgled in his throat and she let up on her grip, but not enough to let him loose. "I can't even imagine what that would be like. *God*. Dead! Was she young?"

"Yeah. I mean, our age. It was hard to tell, but I think so."

Looking through that van window, what had struck me most about the woman was her profile. That's what I thought of while I waited and watched hours of clips, sports scores, repeats of the daily weather report. Her image flickered over top of everything: dark ponytail spilling over the ratty cushion of the minivan's backseat, her lips a soft, sticky red, cheek downy as a ripe peach. The stillness of her chest had unnerved me before I'd even understood what was wrong; the inaction superimposed over a bustling parking lot rammed full of carts and cars. Someone had laid on the horn while we'd peered in the woman's backseat, which had scared me horribly. I'd put a hand up to my chest while Deanna shoved her own buggy out of the way, giving them the middle finger. *Asshole*, she'd yelled in her high, childlike voice. *Everyone's an asshole today.*

The segment aired in the middle of the eleven o'clock news. Marissa had gone to lie down after heating up a rice sack for her back. Samson had followed her out of the room, his broad belly swaying just above the floor. The clip was so brief that I rewound it a few times to understand that was all there would be. The anchor with her blonde cap of hair sat perched behind the desk, a box reading "Worked to Death?" hovering overhead like a dialogue bubble from a comic strip. She passed off the story to a reporter on the scene, an eager young guy with dark, slicked back hair and a bright blue tie. He stood in the empty parking lot, near where I'd parked my sedan just that morning.

Where was the van? I wondered. *Did they haul it to a wrecking yard?*

Her name was Sylvia Rodrigues. The man gestured vaguely to the Dunkin' Donuts on the corner of the lot, noting that the woman held three different part-time jobs in the area. She had a couple of kids, no husband. She was working to help support her elderly parents, who lived out of state and had health problems.

"It's thought that the woman decided to take a nap in the hours between her shifts at Walmart and at this local Dunkin' Donuts. Medical authorities suspect that her body succumbed to the heat while she slept, slipping into the coma that ultimately led to her death."

A picture flashed on screen. I rewound and paused the frame, trying to correlate the two images in my brain—the woman shown on TV and the one I'd seen in the minivan. She had very white teeth and dark eyes that crinkled in the corners. The photo was grainy and looked out of date. I wondered who'd submitted it, if she was all alone, except for the kids. Did she have friends who helped her out? Then the segment was over, and it was time for the weather report again.

"Looks like some rain this week, huh? I could have told you that." Marissa stood behind the couch, rubbing her temples. She got sinus headaches whenever a front came through, and they'd gotten worse with all the pregnancy hormones.

Her stomach was gently rounded at this point—five months along, her first pregnancy, my first pregnancy. We weren't supposed to worry about money, but I did, constantly. Wondered about whether this baby would go to grad school or if it would need braces. How we would pay for things if my wife decided not to go back to work, and from the way she talked, it seemed like she wouldn't.

"Can you pick up doughnuts in the morning?"

"I have a meeting with my clients."

Marissa frowned. "That's not until eleven. I didn't even get cinnamon rolls today." She cupped her belly, thumbs stroking circles at either side of what could be a boy or a girl. We wanted to be surprised.

No reason to say no. "Yes, okay. I'll get them."

Sylvia Rodrigues had one of both, a ten-year-old boy and a six-year-old girl. Maybe they would go into foster care. I wondered if Sylvia usually brought them home doughnuts from work, something sweet to wake up to for breakfast. If she leaned over them in their beds and kissed them goodnight, her breath smelling of coffee and her skin of cooking grease.

The Dunkin' Donuts drive thru had a line that snaked around the building and into the parking lot, nearly blocking off the entrance to the street. The cars idled there, coughing exhaust in tandem, drivers hunched over their steering wheels and creeping along with no end in sight. I took one look at the mess and pulled into the nearest parking spot in front of the grocery store.

Locking the doors, I looked out across the lot to where Sylvia's minivan had sat the day before. A puddle of dark, oily liquid stained the ground. It was the kind stuff that spit and seeped when the air conditioning wasn't running properly. My old car had done that until Marissa took it in for a tune up. I stared at the spot for so long that another person pulled out of the line and into the parking spot beside mine, a mother with an SUV full of children, three of them in car seats. I waved to the kid nearest me, a little blonde boy with tufted hair sucking a pacifier. He stared at me blankly until his mother dragged open the sliding door and pulled the seatbelt over his head.

There were people five deep waiting to order, but only one person behind the counter. I stood at the back of the line and watched the doughnuts plucked from their wire baskets: plain cake, chocolate, seasonal varieties with red, white, and blue candy stars sprinkled across their tops. Sausage biscuits whirled and heated in the industrial microwave. Overlarge plastic containers churned milky frappuccino mixes that people ordered in plastic cups with domed lids. The woman behind the counter filled boxes, stuffed bags with paper napkins, poured coffees with cream and artificial sweetener. She swizzled stir sticks into cups before shoving them into outstretched hands.

Bright red hair frizzed underneath her brown visor. She looked at me expectantly as I approached the counter, brushing powdered sugar fingerprints off the front of her apron. Her nametag read Helen, but the tape that secured the name had peeled up at the back end until it read "Hel."

"What can I get you?"

I looked at what was left and couldn't decide. "Dozen, mixed. Whatever you have left."

The pink and orange boxes were stowed under the counter. She assembled one without looking at it, staring through the plate glass window at the line of cars piled up at the drive-thru window. She carried the box open-faced to the back counter, grabbing a tissue from a nearby bin and rapidly chunking doughnuts into the bottom. A bell dinged in the back. Through the gaps in the doughnut bins, a shadow figure darted toward the window.

"Pretty busy today, huh?" I debated asking for a coffee, even though I knew there would be a full pot waiting at home. There was just something nice about having someone else make it, having them mix in the cream and sugar.

"Yep. We're short staffed."

That was all she said about it, but I noted the missing half to her sentence: short staffed because an employee had passed away very suddenly in the parking lot. Short staffed because Sylvia was never going to make her shift again. Hel handed me the box and I decided to go for the coffee after all, even though I knew Marissa would have something to say about it. As Hel poured and stirred, slipping on the plastic lid, I listened to the grumbles coming from behind me. A car horn sounded in the drive thru, two staccato bursts.

"Are you guys hiring?" I asked.

For the first time, she looked at me. Took in my face—my heavy makeup, my sensible gray business suit with the high-necked blouse. I had a meeting scheduled via Skype in an hour and the top half of me had to look presentable, even though I'd just put my sleep shorts back on and not wear any shoes, unless Marissa asked me to go out and get the mail.

Hel's eyes narrowed. "For your kid? They gotta be eighteen, we need someone to pick up night shift."

"Right." I shook my head. "No. I mean, for me."

She squinted further and I realized she was probably nearsighted. Her eyes were small and deep-set in her pinkly flushed face. She reached beneath the counter and handed me a paper application. I hadn't filled out something like that since I was in high school, working at the ice cream place owned by my best friend's parents. We'd both worked very limited afternoon hours, smoking weed in the back office and eating tiny bites of ice cream from the sample cups when we got hungry. I took my stuff and sat down at a pink and brown booth lodged by one of the front windows. The table was still damp from where someone has swiped at it with a wet rag and the application dampened in one corner. I dragged it to a spot I dried with my sleeve.

Almost everyone who came inside took their stuff to go, in a hurry to get to work or back home. I sipped my coffee slowly and opened the doughnut box, selecting one of the patriotic sprinkled ones. I ate one bite of doughnut for each step of the application: where I lived, my last employer, my social security number. It was relaxing to sit while the world moved around me. My phone buzzed in my purse, but I ignored it. I ate another doughnut, a chocolate cake with sticky glaze that made my hands tacky and coated the pen I was using with sugary dust.

By the time I finished filling out the paper, I'd eaten four doughnuts and the line had dwindled to a single customer waiting for his egg and cheese croissant to finish twirling in the microwave. The front of the store smelled like someone's old running shoes.

I handed the application to Hel and she stared at it blankly. "You could have taken it home, filled it out there."

"I can start as early as tomorrow." I finished the last of the coffee—syrupy-sweet with the dregs of the sugar grainy against my tongue—and tossed it into the trash, which was near to overflowing.

"We'll let you know."

Hel called less than an hour after I left. I was in a meeting with my clients, a married couple who ran a gym. They were arguing over the web page header. The husband wanted something with weights in the image, while the wife was trying to gear it toward stay-at-home moms. It was the same argument they'd had for three weeks. I left them to their squabble and muted myself out of the conversation.

"Would you be able to pick up a night shift tomorrow? I know that's soon, but you said you could and we need someone right away." Hel's voice was tinny over the background noise of traffic. I assumed she was calling me from a cell phone out in the parking lot, maybe around the back where I'd noticed an employee entrance.

I rolled my chair over to the window and looked out to see Marissa clipping the side of one of our large bushes at the side of the house. She was in a one-piece navy bathing suit. With her pregnant belly, she looked a little like that girl from the movie who'd swelled up like a big balloon. "Yeah, that should be fine."

"I've got an extra uniform here. Might be too small, but it's all we've got. I'll put in an order for you after you get here and fill out the rest of the paperwork."

It could have been Sylvia's. Maybe one that she'd left in the store, so she could change in the back, out of her other work clothes. "Okay."

Marissa carried the clippings over to her little green wheelbarrow and dumped them in. As she brushed off her arms, clippings slipped onto the paved walkway and into the pool. I'd have to dig leaves out of the filter. The last time we'd had to call out a specialist to clean it and he'd given us a lecture. *Ladies, you can't just throw whatever in this thing. It's a filter, not a garbage disposal.* He'd smiled as he'd said it, but it bothered me to hear him say "ladies," like I'd go around just throwing banana peels in the pool.

"I guess I'll see you tomorrow night. Call if you change your mind, I can't do another day like today."

"Sure thing." The husband and wife were still arguing, both pixelated and angry on opposite sides of my screen. I couldn't hear what they were saying, but they were making a lot of emphatic arm gestures. They hadn't even noticed I'd left the conversation.

"Can I ask you something?" The sound of a car horn blasted through the phone. I wondered if the drive-thru was backed up again.

"Yeah, of course."

"Why are you doing this? I mean, we need the help, but your references show that you could get something better."

Marissa waded into the pool, slowly, lowering her body into the water until her head disappeared below the window frame. When I looked back to the computer, the husband and wife had finished arguing with each other and were staring at me.

"I need it." I held up my finger to the couple, *just one second*, and the wife's eyes narrowed. They paid me by the hour. "I don't know why, I just do."

"Fine. Don't be late."

Water lapped onto the deck as Marissa suddenly resurfaced, mouth blowing mist as she exhaled. She collected the stray leaves and sticks, piling them at the pool's edge. Then she rolled onto her back and floated to the center of the pool, feet kicking lazily, arms churning white. Her belly poked up from the water like a dark island.

I unmuted myself from the conversation. "So, what did we decide?"

The apron was already stained with someone else's grease. It was too tight in the waist, although maybe I'd just put it on wrong over my khakis. The visor's brim made my hair puff strangely from the top of my head, resembling a mushroom's cap. I thought Marissa would laugh if she could see me, but she wouldn't. She thought I'd gone to book club.

Hel walked me around the front of the store, showing me how to work the register, talking to me about the process for operating the drive-thru.

"Late night menu's pretty basic, see?" Hel pointed to the illuminated sign—orders were limited to beverages and hot sandwiches, plus the ever-replenishing doughnuts. The whole store smelled like powdered sugar and leftover cooking oil, making me feel hungry and sick.

Sylvia worked nights and manned the counter, probably dozing under the humming buzz of the overhead fluorescents. My eyes felt dry and wanted to close against the electric brightness of the place. I wondered how often employees must have curled up in the sticky vinyl booths and just gone to sleep, waiting for the ding of the alert to let them know someone was waiting in the drive-thru.

"Hey. *Hey.*"

Hel was glaring at me, eyes narrowed into pie slits in her doughy face. I realized she must have been talking to me the whole time I'd been zoning out.

"Could you repeat that?" I asked.

"I said there are a lot of other people who could use this job, people with bills they gotta pay." With her arms crossed, I could make out dense lines of muscle beneath the freckled flesh.

"I'm sorry," I said. "I'll do better."

"If I didn't need someone right away, I wouldn't have hired you." She jerked her thumb toward the back. "Go get the mop and clean up, the whole front and behind the counters."

"Right. Sorry."

Her face softened. "The good thing about this job is you get all the free coffee you want. You drink coffee?"

"Yeah, I'd love some."

Hel pulled one of the big plastic travel mugs from beneath the counter and filled it from the oversized metal coffee urn. "This one's yours now. Just bring it back with you, fill up whenever you want. Cream, sugar. Whatever. We even have those flavored syrups, if you're into that."

We spent the rest of the evening manning separate parts of the store. I cleaned up the back with the big mop and bucket, redolent of Clorox. The scent reminded me of the janitors in grade school when they'd had to mop up messes—spilled milk or vomit. Kids overflowing with fluids, all the time. Messy children that had no idea how their own bodies operated.

As I mopped, methodically, slipping the wet head from one corner to the other, I thought of Sylvia. How had she mopped the floor? Diagonally? Without thought for the task, maybe thinking of the next job she had to run to? About her kids at home, waiting in bed, wondering when their mom would be home to tuck them in? The pattern on the floor was alternating squares of beige, interspersed with a chocolate brown the exact color of my apron. I took sips of coffee every third swipe, the caffeine carrying me to a dizzy place that put me on edge. My phone buzzed in my pocket, again and again, and I ignored it, moving the wheeled bucket with my foot, slopping dirty water down into my socks.

"Can you pour me two large cokes?" Hel leaned back from the window. "Bring them to customers while I grab a dozen."

The coke machine slurped cold fizz into the large paper cups. I pressed on the lids and carried them over to the window, opening the glass doors and letting in the heat and damp. The car was lower than the sill, and I had to lean through the window to pass them to the hands stretched up from the driver's seat. It was a car full of teenaged guys, indistinguishable from each other in the dark, except for the driver. He had close-cropped hair and wore a red and black Bucs jersey.

"Straws?" he asked. The stubble on his chin competed with the white-capped acne.

"Right! Sorry, let me get those." I could hear Hel constructing the paper box for the doughnuts, the flip and slide of the thick paper against the countertop. I grabbed a couple paper wrapped straws from the dispenser and headed back to the window. Leaning through, I saw the wide mouth of the cup was open. The lid was in his other hand.

Soda doused my face and head, the cold sweetness splashing in my mouth. I yelled, a strangled half-shout, half-yelp. As the car squealed past, the boys inside hooted and laughed. Ice rained down the collar of my shirt and into the front of my apron.

Hel ran in, took look at me, and ran back out. I followed her.

"Fucking animals!" Her face was smashed against the glass. When she looked back at me, there was a greasy print in the shape of her cheek smudging the window. "I got half their license number this time."

Coke was dripping all over the floor I'd just mopped. Soaking through my shirt and pants. My ear began to feel numb, and I realized that ice was lodged in the crown of my visor. I threw it off and it skittered across the tile, sliding beneath the cash register. I shook off like a dog, walking into the back to wash my hands and face in the bathroom sink. After a minute of scrubbing, I dunked my head under the tap, too, just to rinse the stickiness from my hair.

Hel was mopping the floor when I emerged, wet and bedraggled.

"I can get that," I said, but she ignored me.

"This is maybe the fourth time this year those little pricks have done this." Her face was red and sweaty. She shoved the mop across the floor, throwing it back and forth, a near chokehold on the handle. "They got Sylvia last month. Someone posted a video on the internet."

"Sylvia?" This was the first I'd heard anyone speak of her; someone who actually knew her.

"Sylvia Rodriguez. You probably saw on the news, she died in her car last week waiting for her shift." Hel shook her head, mopped harder. The muscles on her arms stood out in angry, stark lines. "Dying in your car, waiting for some stupid job you don't give a shit about that won't even pay for groceries."

"I'm sorry."

Hel dumped the mop back into the bucket. "At least she got some rest."

I remembered what it had looked like to see a woman sleeping in a car like that, the sweat making her hair cling to her neck. How the dampness made her skin looked soft and dewy, the same sweet sugary texture of a doughnut.

On the drive home, I shifted uncomfortably against the collar of the sticky uniform and watched the glowing gas stations zip past with their bright white lights and smudged concrete. The world felt hollow and empty, everyone mostly asleep, except for the few of us out driving carefully in the center of our lanes. In that dark span of time between waking and sleeping, my whole body was jittery and ill at ease, as if it knew what it was doing was wrong—a computer overriding the natural state of things, my brain was programmed to slide into unconsciousness.

I showered and fell into our bed, disrupting the cat. He mewled pitifully and wandered out to the living room while I bundled in behind my wife, trying to calm my shivering body. Marissa had left the bedroom curtain cracked, and some light from a street lamp puddled yellow on the floor by the side of the bed. I sat up and rubbed at my right shoulder, which throbbed in the socket, aching like it was ready to pull loose. Mopping the floors had left my muscles tender and wobbly, like gelatin that wouldn't set properly. I was embarrassed. I couldn't remember the last time my body hurt like that, as if it were punishing me for not working harder.

We needed a new mattress. The movement of my body rolled Marissa over into the deep groove in the middle. She rubbed at her back constantly, the pressure from the baby inside already pulling hard on the muscles at either side of her spine. Light from the window etched a wide white curve into her forehead. She looked very young, the glow smoothing out the tender, pale skin around her eyes. We had not touched much lately. Every time she came close to me, pressed a hand to my face, or rubbed fingers across my arm, I shut down, as if there was something in me that couldn't bear skin-to-skin contact. She rolled over again in the bed, her hair spilling down between our pillows in a dark river.

It was no use staying in the room. Marissa was already murmuring something, on the cusp of waking, too, and she'd never get back to sleep. I got up and went out through the hall, leaving off all the lights. The door opened smoothly as I walked out of the house and onto the back porch.

There were noises puncturing the night air, crackles in the trees overhead, and sharp scrapes against the pavement that could have been pets or wild animals. Maybe a possum trying to dig into our trash. I wanted to go back inside the house, to lie down beside my wife, but I couldn't make my mind shut down. I walked around the side of the house, barefoot, in only my sleep shorts and sports bra. The grass felt terrible beneath my feet, crunchy and full of dead things. Out front the cars sat, side-by-side, bathed in the lemon-yellow lamplight from the street. My car was locked, but Marissa's was open. She had a shiny black SUV, purchased two months ago, back when she'd decided we should be sport utility moms.

All noise ceased when I closed the car door behind me. It felt like a vacuum; my own breath harsh in my head. I lay down flat, the center belt buckle digging into my hipbone. My muscles hurt. I turned onto my side and shut my eyes, envisioning what the morning would look like from the inside of the car, looking out at the sun from beneath dark tint.

Shadows flickered through my closed lids, and then there was a sharp tap against the glass. I sat up choking on air, my wife's shape taking up the window. She opened the car door and the humidity spilled inside with me as she reached in and pulled me upright. My knees touched her stomach. Her sleep shirt was worn through—an old relic from a trip to the Bahamas with her parents after she graduated high school.

"What is this?" she asked, wrapping my arms around her waist. "Are you okay?"

Her belly sat between us like a warm lump of dough. I strained my own stomach against it, to see if I could feel movement, something tangible that could root me in the moment that already felt dreamy and disconnected from reality.

"I'm just tired," I said. Her eyes were wide and scared. I kissed her cheek, rubbed my thumb across her bottom lip. "I don't know what I'm doing."

"Please come back inside. Come back to bed."

"I can't sleep." I said. My eyes were hot and my cheeks throbbed. "My brain won't shut off."

Marissa led me back to the house, this time through the front door. Back into our bedroom with the light spilling through the curtain. I crawled up on the mattress, felt the weight of her dip behind me. She pulled the sheet up over our bodies as our legs tangled together. Her belly pressed against my back, a solid, reassuring weight. The baby nestled between us; I covered her body with my own, protecting everyone while I could.

The Locusts

The cousins gathered acorns beneath the wide canopy of oak trees, filling up the pockets of their shirts and pants until they bulged. Though there were hundreds carpeting the ground behind their grandparent's house, they kept only the unblemished ones, tossing out any that were punctured or hollow. They pried off the acorn's caps and rubbed their thumbs across the smooth surfaces. Sometimes they broke them open and poked at the swollen orange kernels, imagining what it would be like to eat them. The kids did this every summer, and their parents had done it before them. The grandparent's had owned the house for over thirty years. Before houses had sprouted up, there'd been orange groves bordered by patchy dirt roads and fields full of wild grasses.

The youngest cousin, Charlie, would sometimes roll whole acorns around in his mouth. He sucked on them like peppermints. Brandy was the oldest, and when she saw Charlie do it, she smacked him on the back.

"Don't be gross," she said. "What if a dog peed on that?"

Charlie spat the acorn out in his palm. It was glistening and fat, shiny with spit, and the shell was dented from the bite of his molars. He dropped it on the ground where one day it would grow into a tree that dumped out more acorns for the kids, or maybe just be eaten by a squirrel.

How it worked with the cousins was this: the eldest held the responsibility of looking after all of the younger kids, but they also chose what games they played and made up all the rules. Brandy was the undeclared leader of their group. She wasn't really the oldest cousin; there were two teenaged girls who lived in Atlanta, but she was the oldest in the yard, and that's what mattered. Brandy had just turned eleven, which gave her a three-month advantage over Austin and Shelby, the ten-year-old twins from upstate. There was also six-year-old Charlie. Brandy didn't want to play with a cousin half her age, especially one as obnoxious as Charlie, but her mother had told her to *be nice* in a voice that meant *be nice or else*, so Brandy kept her mouth shut.

That weekend most of the relatives were down visiting from different parts of the state. Aunts and uncles put out the folding tables and dragged dining room chairs into the yard. Brandy's father barbecued, grilling burgers and hot dogs alongside pork tenderloin and porterhouse steaks swirled with rings of fat. The air was thick with the scent of smoked meat and trampled grass. While the adults finished up their potato salad, they drank pulpy lemonade and sweet tea that Brandy's grandmother had made with cane sugar. They digested their food and talked about previous summers, back when they'd run around without any supervision and swum naked in the lake and Brandy's mother had said *remember that time Uncle Jimmy stepped on a rusty nail in the shed and his foot swelled up three times its normal size?*

Brandy couldn't sit still for these stories. She'd heard them over and over again, the emphasis always placed on the same words: Great Aunt Vivian with the *blue hair* and the Pomeranian she'd pushed around in a *baby carriage*, or the arm that Uncle Wilbur's had lost *in the war* that was replaced with a *hook*. They were ghost people who only showed up in old family photos, relatives whose voices she imagined all sounded like her grandparents. When she got antsy enough to start playing with a leftover hamburger bun, her mother let her leave the table, but told her to stay in the yard. Brandy gathered up the rest of the kids and huddled with them in the old doghouse at the edge of the property.

Inside the doghouse smelled like sweaty skin and mildew, but there was also the scent of something tart and metallic, like a ring of keys held in a sweaty fist. It came from a rusty tea set that was kept in an old potato chip can. The set was very old. Brandy's mother had played with them when she was a little girl, and so had Brandy's grandmother. All the cups were rough around the lip, chewed up and pitted. If you drank from them you might cut yourself or wind up with a beard of orange-red dust.

Everything felt more secretive and exciting in a space where their words echoed back at them off the rotten wood. Four kids breathing in each other's oxygen and tasting each other's lunch on their breaths. Brandy's grandparents hadn't owned a dog since Uncle Ronnie's had gotten run over by a delivery truck out in front of the house, a hound dog named Blue who was the color of pewter. Brandy barely remembered that dog, but she knew from stories that he'd always slept at the foot of the staircase and the adults tripped over him all the time. Once her grandma had almost *broke her goddamn neck.*

The kids had stolen two beers from the cooler; a big white Igloo that her grandparents kept especially for family picnics. The cooler sat in the side yard, in the shade, near where the uncles always parked their trucks. Those trucks had big wheels that you could climb on and the beds were always full of things to pick up, like small chunks of scrap metal and empty shell casings from the Uncle's hunting rifles. Brandy was very interested in guns and all kinds of weapons. Her grandfather kept a collection of knives on his dresser among stacks of loose change, and Brandy loved to click them open and closed. Her favorite was a mother-of-pearl handle that shone blue-green when you tilted it in the light. Last year she'd been looking at it and heard her mother calling for her from the other room. She'd sliced a neat line down her palm when she'd tried to close it back up again in a hurry. The cut hurt, but she'd hid her blood from her mother by clutching a fistful of t-shirt behind her back.

The beers left rings on the wood in the center of their circle, two wet eyes goggling at the cousins from the warped floorboards. Brandy knew all about beer. Her father and uncles drank it with their shirts off while they did yard work or when they got together with friends and watched NASCAR racing. The smell was yeasty and fuzzy and almost happy, like when her father got home from long days outside. It reminded Brandy of the breath-smell that happened when her uncles had tossed her up in the air and caught her, their fingers digging into her ribcages. Brandy was too big now for that kind of thing, but the Uncles still threw Charlie. He always cried afterward and said it scared him and hurt his sides.

"I'm gonna open one."

"Don't do it." Shelby said. "Bad idea."

"I'm gonna." Brandy rubbed her finger in the condensation and then tasted it. "I'm gonna do it."

The can hissed when she jammed her fingernail beneath the tab. She didn't open it all the way at first, just a sliver, enough to release the smell. Then she cracked it all the way and the sound was loud enough to make her jump. The kids all huddled around her and stared down into the opening, the liquid clear and bubbly as soda.

"Looks like ginger ale," Austin said, reaching for the can. "Cool."

Brandy pulled it out of his reach. "We're gonna try some."

"Not me," Shelby said. "You guys do it."

"Yes, you. All of us."

Condensation slipped between Brandy's fingers and fell down onto her legs in cold splashes. She held the can up to her face and licked the rim. A watery chunk of ice caught on her front tooth and gave her a chill. Then she tipped her head back and let some of the beer slip into her mouth. The carbonation was high and the fizz burned her throat, and the flavor was like moldy bread. She feigned a large, exaggerated swallow and passed the can to Austin. Then she wiped at her mouth and smiled.

"It's good. Now you."

Austin took a swallow, and then Shelby, who complained that the bubbles hurt her nose and that it tasted like something died, and then Charlie held the can and looked at Brandy. He was small for his age, everyone said so, but he'd been born two months premature. Brandy remembered visiting him in the hospital. He'd been sleeping in a clear plastic incubator, swaddled in a white flannel blanket and wearing a blue hat that her Grandma had knitted in a hurry. She'd been expecting something cute, like a puppy or a kitten, but Charlie had looked wrinkled and mottled-pink and ugly. Her mother said one day he'd catch up with everybody else, but for now his limbs were thin and pale, and he got tired whenever he rode his bike too far out into the neighborhood. The only thing that really grew on Charlie was his hair. It was white-blonde and thick and it curled up in pretty ringlets around his ears. Brandy's own hair was thin and tangled and brown, and nobody ever wanted to play with it, not like they did Charlie's, and he was a boy.

He held up the can, then frowned and set it back down in his lap. "I don't wanna do it."

"Do you want to stay in here with us? Or do you want to go back out and sit with your momma?"

Brandy didn't like how Charlie's eyes were blue. Hers were just plain brown. Her grandmother doted over Charlie; even the aunts thought he was precious, and the uncles gave him rides in their trucks because he was a boy. She knew it was because he was the youngest, but he was also the prettiest, and that didn't feel fair. It didn't matter as much that Shelby had such nice clothes and long hair—the twins lived out of town, so it was fun when they came to visit, like a pretty friend she could play with and borrow things from, one who would go away after the long weekend and not be back for a while. Charlie lived right nearby in a big house with a swimming pool. His nails were always clean and he had a brand new bike with a bell on it.

"Don't make him," Shelby said. She threw an arm around his thin shoulders and Charlie huddled into her side. "He's too little."

"It's no big deal." Austin took another sip. "It tastes fine."

Brandy noticed that he held his lips in a tight line and when he swallowed he looked uncomfortable, like he had a sore throat.

"It smells bad." Charlie's small nose wrinkled. It was what Brandy's mother called a pug nose, and it had tiny freckles sprinkled across it.

"Of course it smells bad, don't be dumb." Brandy took the can from Austin and pretended to take another sip. More slipped into her mouth and soured her tongue. Spit pooled until she was forced to swallow it down, too. Brandy thought it was like drinking someone's backwash. It tasted coppery like blood.

She pushed the can back into Charlie's hand. Brandy smiled at him, her teeth crowded in her mouth from where the new ones were coming in over the old ones. Her sharp baby canines hadn't rocked loose yet, even though she constantly worked at them, and the bigger adult ones were pushing out over top of them. One had already burst through her gums like a vampire's fang. The kids at school always made fun of her teeth; they called her snaggletooth and said she was too poor to go to the dentist. Brandy saw Charlie looking at that tooth and it made her want to bite him.

"Is it 'cause your daddy won't drink it?" she asked. "Is that why?"

"No, I just don't like it."

"You haven't even tried it yet."

Charlie's daddy didn't drink beer. He was the only uncle who chose cans of Coke from the big cooler when all the other uncles drank from silver Coors cans and sweaty brown bottles with labels peeling off in strips. Brandy's mother had told her that Uncle Davey liked beer a little too much when he was younger, so much that he'd drank up all his portion and now he had to save the rest for everyone else.

"It's cause of your daddy," Austin said, smiling. "He's a drunk, that's why."

"Stop it." Shelby shifted on her knees, ready to bolt. "You're gonna make him cry and then we'll get in trouble."

Brandy didn't want to get in trouble, either, but something about the way Charlie acted always made her angry. How he cried at almost everything and how the uncles and aunts all coddled him and picked him up. How all he had to do was smile or sing amazing grace—even finishing his dinner got him praised like a baby genius. Charlie's eyes were already filling up and his face looked puffy and red.

"Listen, it's fine." Brandy wiped at the snot under Charlie's nose and scrubbed it off on the cuff of her jean shorts. "You want to stay in here with us, don't you?"

"Yes . . . "

"Then just take a little sip." Brandy rubbed small circles on Charlie's back, just like her momma did whenever she got bad hiccups. "It won't hurt you. You'll probably like it, I bet."

Charlie's ribs poked through his t-shirt like piano keys and her fingers pressed down between the bones. She smoothed her hands up and down to keep from squeezing too hard. His shirt rose up and down off his back; it was close in the doghouse and her hands were sweaty and so was the skin of his back.

She guided the can up to his mouth and Charlie took a taste. Brandy smoothed her hand up and down again and smiled over Charlie's head at Austin and Shelby. The two looked relieved and huddled into each other. Brandy didn't know what they were so worried about. As far as she knew, her cousins never got in trouble for anything. They always had new clothes and their mom never yelled at them in front of company, not anything like Brandy's parents. Charlie took another sip.

"Not so bad, huh?"

Charlie shook his head. The can was still icy cold and Brandy thought it looked just like it always did in the commercials, those ones with the people running around smiling under a big yellow butterball of sunshine, kicking up sand on the beach, their hair long and pretty. Brandy opened the other can and took a small sip, just to feel the cold on her tongue. It didn't taste as bad as it did before. She took another sip and then another. The fuzz licked at the roof of her mouth.

She passed the can to Austin and he took a long gulp. Shelby just sat there and looked grumpy. Brandy thought she didn't look as pretty with her curly hair all frizzed from the humidity. There was a big dirt smudge across the front of her white shirt, and Brandy knew that the dirt was probably mixed with rust, and that meant the stain wouldn't come out. The shirt had ruffled sleeves and pearly buttons at the neck. She wondered if maybe Shelby's mom would give Brandy's mom that shirt and maybe some other clothes too, like how she sometimes did when they came to visit. They'd bring a big plastic garbage bag full of clothes that Shelby didn't want anymore, or that had stains, or that maybe didn't fit right or had scratchy lace on them. Brandy would wear those clothes to school and it didn't matter that the pants would be too short by a few inches, because they were the nicest clothes she'd ever owned. Not like stuff her mother bought from Kmart that always fit wrong.

"Not too much," Brandy said. She took the can from Charlie and set it back down on the floor.

Charlie's eyes were glassy and wide. Brandy felt sleepy and leaned back against the wooden wall of the doghouse, the splinters digging into her back and poking through her t-shirt. The feel of it rough against her back combined with a buildup of sweat made her feel itchy.

"Let's get another one." Austin drained the last few sips. The empty can made a flat, hollow sound when he set it back down on the wood. It tipped over sideways and rolled into Brandy's leg. She let it lie there, against her skin, feeling the warmed up condensation.

"No, I don't wanna get caught." Shelby was sitting half out of the doghouse with the heels of her white sneakers dragging through the dirt. They were brand new. When she picked one up to dust it off, the color was pale gray.

"I'm gonna get a coke," Austin said. "This is boring."

Shelby trailed Austin across the yard and Brandy leaned out to watch them go, thinking that she might like a coke, but she was pretty tired. Then she leaned back inside the doghouse and sat down across from Charlie. The space was more comfortable now that it was just the two of them; Brandy could stretch her legs out a little bit. Charlie looked relaxed, too. His eyes were sleepy slits and his cheeks were bright pink. Every few seconds his tongue slipped out and wet his lips, as if he could still taste the beer. Brandy picked up the remaining can and took another swallow. It wasn't as cold as before. The heat had made it go flat, and now it tasted like she was sucking water from a bath sponge. Charlie reached for the can and she let him take it, watched his eyes close up as he took long, slow swallows. A little of the beer dribbled from the corner of his mouth and landed on the front of his shirt—a button-up oxford with rolled sleeves that looked limp and deflated, not crisp like when he'd worn it to the church service earlier that morning.

"I hate these plates." Brandy took a stack of them from the potato chip can. "They're so ugly." They had pictures of Raggedy Ann and Andy on the front of them, though most of the faces had scrubbed off until all you could see were fuzzy clouds of red yarn hair. Brandy took the beer and poured the rest of it into one of the rusty cups. Dirt pooled up across the top of the yellow liquid, looking like when dogs peed yellow streams in the grass. She handed it to Charlie and he took sips from it until he'd drained about half the cup.

"It's so hot out here, I can't stand it," she said. "It feels like I'm being smothered."

A strand of hair was across her throat and the sweat made it cling like a necklace. Charlie was pulling acorns from his pants pockets and rubbed them between his fingers. Brandy took hers out too, and then they piled them in one of the saucers that went with the play set. The acorns rolled around in a big pile, dark marbles that shifted smoothly across the plate. When Brandy squinted they looked like chocolate drops, or maybe like bugs.

"Locusts," she said. "They look like locusts." They'd talked about the plagues of Egypt in Sunday School that morning. The plagues were all terrible. There were the rivers of coppery blood, and dead livestock with their throats dried up from thirst, or the firstborn children struck down by an awful angel of death. To Brandy, nothing could compare to an infestation of bugs. Mrs. Madison had asked her to imagine finding them in your cereal when you overturned the box, or to think about them crawling inside your mouth when you were trying to sleep. That's what had happened in ancient Egypt. She'd said the locust babies had hatched in the Egyptians' ears, nested inside their shoes, had eaten big holes in their clothes and camped out inside their bed sheets. The Egyptians had to deal with all of those locusts just because Pharaoh wouldn't let God's people go, but Brandy thought that meant that the Israelites had to deal with all those things, too. Fulfilling God's promises always meant sacrifice. That's what Brandy's mother said when she made Brandy tithe ten percent of her allowance every Sunday. Her quarters falling in the collection plate for mission trips to countries she'd never even heard of or seen on a map.

Brandy didn't actually know what locusts looked like, but she thought maybe they were like roaches.

"I'm hungry," Charlie said. "And thirsty."

"Why didn't you finish your lunch?"

"Didn't like it. Don't like hot dogs."

"You don't like anything."

Charlie was a really picky eater. He would poke at his dinner and lunches, and the grownups never made him finish anything. Not like Brandy, whose father made her sit at the table long after everyone else had gone off to do other things. He'd set the timer on the oven for fifteen minutes, and if Brandy didn't finish everything on her plate she got a swat on the leg that usually left a red mark. Then she was embarrassed and upset and she still had to eat whatever was left.

"Hungry." He rubbed his stomach and flapped his arms to try and get comfortable. Brandy thought he looked like a baby bird.

"Close your eyes," she said. "And open wide."

Brandy chose an acorn from the dish on Charlie's lap and pushed it into his mouth. His eyes opened wide as his throat worked and he swallowed the whole thing down in one gulp.

Brandy smiled. "Want another?"

Charlie opened his mouth and she pushed the second inside. She laughed and he grinned hugely at her. His mouth was wet and red, and there was a small patch of dirt stuck to one of his front teeth. She hugged him as he sipped from the teacup, sucking down more floating dirt and lukewarm beer.

"Good job, buddy. Again?"

He nodded and put one in his mouth. When he swallowed it, she rubbed his back and then ran her fingers through his sweaty hair. It stuck up in electric white peaks and she giggled and thought he looked sweet. Her very own pet bird with his small nose and his sweet fat cheeks. If baby birds ate bugs, then baby birds could eat locusts. Brandy thought that maybe if Moses had brought out a flight of birds, the locusts would have all been eaten up. Maybe that's what God had done to get rid of them, maybe that was how he'd protected the Israelites. Hungry birds perched all around their slave quarters, scavenging for insects.

"You're like a cute little baby," Brandy said. "Like a pretty doll."

Charlie's eyes were heavily lashed and his round cheeks were flushed and sticky from the heat. When his mouth dropped open, Brandy could see a little bit of drool leak out and wet his chin. She wondered if he'd let her dress him up in some of the old baby clothes in the attic—there were bonnets and old christening dresses, stuff turning yellow and crunchy that nobody would miss.

"How many can you eat?" Brandy asked. "One more?"

Charlie shoved a fistful of acorns into his mouth and swallowed hard. Then he sat straight up, scrambling around and knocking into Brandy as he tried to climb over her and out of the doghouse.

"Charlie, you're hurting me." Brandy pushed him, but he lashed out with his right arm and it hit her in the face. Pain burned in her cheek and chin, and she tasted blood from where her teeth had sliced into her lower lip. She yelled and shoved him through the doorway until he was laid out flat on his back in the yard. He writhed around, his head digging into the soft ground until his bright hair was crowned with leaves and dirt.

"Stop it!" Brandy yelled. "I'm going to tell your momma you hit me and you're gonna get in trouble."

He thrashed and clawed at his throat, his sneakers kicking up dirt that launched onto her clothes. Brandy kneeled down next to him and took both of his wrists in her hands and tried to pin them to the ground, but his body was surprisingly strong and wiry. He struggled violently beneath her and when his lips parted, she saw an acorn perched at the back of his throat. It disappeared with the next swallow.

Brandy dug down into his mouth to try and reach it, rooting around at the back of his throat, but there was only his tongue and slick, spitty skin. His molars clamped down onto her fingers and his jaw locked into place. There wasn't pain at first, just hard pressure cracking down on her knuckle, and immediate anxiety that he'd try to swallow her finger along with the acorn. When his mouth opened again and she saw blood coating her hand, she was the one who screamed.

She screamed until her throat felt raw. Then their family surrounded them, a mass of uncles and aunts, and one them picked her up off of Charlie and shoved her across the grass until she fell down onto her knees.

Brandy's mother caught her hand and yanked her to her feet. "What is it, what happened?"

"I don't know!" Brandy's fingers throbbed and she shook them.

"What's wrong with him?" She grabbed Brandy's hand and examined the blood. "Is he hurt?"

She couldn't see Charlie. Her mother peered down at her and Brandy blinked and tried to look away, and then her mother shook her, hard, until her teeth clacked together. Her mother's eyes were brown, like Brandy's, but the whites swam with red squiggles and there was a yellow crust in one of the corners, as if she'd just woken up from a nap. "Did you hurt him?"

She couldn't speak. Her mother saw all of her at once, like when she was six years old and took the chocolate syrup out of the cabinet and smeared it across the rug in the middle of the living room—and she hadn't needed to tell on herself, because the dark streaks of her fingerprints told the story for her. When her Uncle picked up Charlie's body, his legs dangled limp and pale white across the skin of her uncle's tanned forearms, and Brandy's blood painted his cheek.

Charlie's mother was making a high, keening noise that made Brandy want to start screaming again, but her throat had closed up and she could barely pull in air. Then everyone was running around the side of the house to the cars except for Brandy and her mother, whose nails dug down into the muscle of her arm. Someone shouted something, words Brandy couldn't make out, and her mother loosened her grip. Brandy broke free and ran.

She bolted through the fence at the back gate. She didn't stop running until she was three blocks away, until she'd reached the chain link fence by the house with the Japanese plum tree that hung low over the sidewalk; the tree with the fruit that the kids liked to eat when it got perfectly ripe and dark orange. She didn't take any, but she still kept walking, kept propelling herself forward down the streets behind her grandparent's neighborhood. There were people in driveways and sitting on their porches, and a man washing his car with a big red bucket full of soap, and sometimes they waved at her and sometimes they didn't, but Brandy just kept walking. If she stopped, she worried everything would just start hurting again.

The lake at the end of the long block was reedy and full of weeds. Once her grandma had walked all the grandkids down there as a group and they'd seen a coral snake, tangled up in the cattails at the edge of the water where the mud started to suck at Brandy's shoes. Perched high and swaying in the breeze, it was the one bright thing in a kingdom of garbage. Her grandma said the lake was a place where teenagers hung out at night and drank, even though the sign said no loitering after sundown, and they liked to throw their trash in the lake. The whole time her grandma had talked about the teenagers and the garbage and the drinking, the snake hadn't moved, just hung from one of the fuzzy tops where down had begun to fly free. She'd wanted to touch it so badly; the jeweled skin shiny and slick. She'd imagined the heft of it would feel like a warmed-over sequined evening bag, like the kind her mother wore out for special occasions. The snake had perched there, motionless, and she'd stared at its black eyes and wanted to know what it felt like to live life in a skin that was constantly shedding.

There was a picnic table half-sunk in the muck next to the water from where the summer rain had slopped it into the dirt and weeds. Brandy sat on top of it and looked at her fingers. The skin around her knuckles was rubbed raw, and there was an open dent on the side, as if the flesh had vanished. When she squeezed her hand into a fist, blood oozed out and she rubbed it off on the table. It left a dark brown streak in the shape of a crescent.

A car horn sounded down the street and Brandy crawled underneath the table and curled up beside one of the benches. She prayed for Charlie to be okay again, hoped that when he woke up he wouldn't tell on her. She kept thinking of his throat, how when he swallowed the acorns she'd seen them hanging black at the back of his tongue—how it had looked like the locusts were choking him. Brandy wrapped her arms around her legs and hid her face in her knees. She rubbed her forehead against the fuzz of dark incoming hair that her mother wouldn't let her shave yet, and she felt the air get cooler and knew that it was sundown.

Noise came and went from the street. There was a dog howling and a man yelled for him to shut up in an angry voice, but the dog just kept on yelping. Brandy shrank down further beneath the bench, worried about the teenagers that her grandma had talked about, but no one came down to where she squatted beneath the picnic table. Aside from the sound of cars driving past, there was the low hum of frogs and animals scurrying in the water. There were mosquitoes out this time of year, thick swarms of them, and Brandy quickly grew tired of slapping at them and just let them bite.

There was a paper bag beneath the table. Brandy opened it and saw there was a big glass beer bottle inside it, the kind that Brandy's dad bought sometimes after finishing up a double shift down at the construction site. The smell made Brandy feel queasy. She'd left the beer cans sitting inside the doghouse, the empty cans that they'd finished—maybe they were still there and no one had looked yet? Maybe she could throw them away without anyone knowing what she'd done?

Brandy burrowed down inside the neck of her t-shirt and pulled in her arms and legs, stretching it out until her knees were poking out like giant bony breasts. The fabric was musty and sweaty, but she felt more comfortable in her self-made cocoon. She was so tired from the beer and the heat, but she didn't want to go home, didn't want to get in trouble with her parents over what had happened with Charlie. She lay down in the piled dirt beneath the table, curling an arm beneath her head as fish splashed out in the dark water and the cicadas rattled overhead.

When she finally slept, Brandy dreamed of the coral snake. The stripes coiled and uncoiled, illuminating the sky with blinks of red and yellow, red and yellow, like dry lightning. When the flashes hit, they floodlit the pale skin of a tree trunk—except when the light flashed again, it wasn't a tree at all. It was Charlie's neck, and the snake was wrapped tight around it, writhing and hissing, constricting deep into the flesh. The sly flick of the snake's tongue brushed against his cheek as Charlie's eyes bulged into unseeing nothing.

In the dream she couldn't move, but when Charlie's mouth finally opened, Brandy could see the locusts. Out of the darkness, a plague boiled over his lips until they flew at her. They climbed into her clothes and shoes, crawled in her hair, turning her limbs into a roiling mass of their dark, thick bodies. She couldn't shake them off. When she opened her mouth to scream, one of the locusts crawled inside and sat on her tongue.

Morning sunlight sliced into the skin of the lake, burning through the cracks in the picnic table and shining into her eyes, waking her with a jolt. Her fist was lodged at the base of her neck. When she unclenched her fingers they felt cramped, as if she'd been holding onto loose change for too long and the bones in her hand remembered the shape. Brandy's head hurt from where she'd lain on top of a broken stick and there was dirt lining her nostrils from where she'd breathed in silt. Her fingers drew tracks along her face when she dug the crust from her eyes.

Brandy's stomach swam. When she crawled from beneath the picnic table, there was garbage scattered along the ground near where she'd slept, and she tripped over the empty bottle of beer, broken on the ground, and when she stepped on it with her sneaker it cracked underneath her heel. There was a snapping turtle sitting at the edge of the reeds. Brandy stretched her arms up over her head, and it skittered backwards into the water and disappeared with a flat splash. Her shorts were twisted and there was a raw zipper burn from where it had pressed a deep groove into her hip while she was sleeping.

Her neck hurt. She remembered her dream about Charlie and wondered if it meant he was dead. Her eyes burned as she stared unblinking at the water until the lake turned into a pool of shiny glitter. She sat on top of the picnic table as the sun slowly moved through the clouds coming on fat with rain, running her fingernail along the dark place where her blood had dried. Her nail came back caked with dirt and gunk, and she walked down to the water to wash her hands. There were small minnows circling, zipping silver over empty glass bottles and cloudy hunks of algae. While she rinsed, a car pulled up at the edge of the street. Her mother climbed out and ran to her, slipping awkwardly in the damp grass. Brandy thought she'd never seen her mother look so wild or unsure before, her hair frizzy and haloing her head, face red and splotchy from crying.

When her mother caught her in her arms, Brandy felt her throat close up. There were acorns all around the wooden picnic table and they rolled under her sneakers as she was led toward the car, her mother's arms wrapped tight around her ribcage. They did not speak. She climbed into the passenger seat and buckled her seatbelt, and her mother did the same. Then her mother took a stack of fast food napkins from the glove box and used her spit to rub the dried blood from Brandy's face. Brandy held the dirty napkins in her lap as her mother started the car and drove the opposite direction from her grandparent's house, toward home.

Playing Fetch

When you can't sleep, it helps to go on the internet.

In the stark, clean glow of your computer screen, you watch the little girl talk through a mouth full of crackers. Her fuzzy baby hair haloes her head a brilliant golden-white. She's speaking about love, the dynamic of love, although she isn't using grown up words to do it. That's what makes it funny. The words and the mouth full of cracker.

Here's what you know from the caption: the girl is nearly three years old in this video, but she looks much younger than that. She rocks back and forth on the carpet, in front of her father's knee. The knee is dark and hairy. You can hear his voice, but it's disembodied. It comes from the dark, hairy kneecap. The little girl touches that knee and then folds over and touches her own head to the carpet. She laughs with her face pressed into the nap, and the sound is like someone talking underwater. When her head comes up again, there are cracker bits smeared on the floor. The girl holds a doll, and the doll's head flops backward on its neck like a broken flower stem. The woman holding the camera laughs and the camera shakes. You hear her voice too, but it's also displaced. It's a higher pitched twin of the daughter.

The daughter says, "Daddy is very sweet."

The daughter says, "Daddy loves you. Daddy misses you."

Why are you watching this again? The parents laugh and repeat the daughter's words as she touches her father's knee and then presses her face into the carpet. The computer screen glows striking blue against your face as you watch this video. It hollows divots into your cheeks and carves a jawline from stone. It draws a sharp goatee on your chin, like a villain dressed in black who's tied other people's daughters to the train tracks. The little girl laughs and pushes her face into the carpet. The film loops and loops again, a scene that repeats itself every thirty seconds, as if it forgets what was shown moments before and needs everyone to look again.

Only half a minute, but you recognize every scene. Two parents, one child. It plays until everything is marked by the formation of the little girl's language, by the ordering of vowels and consonants. It loops until time is reflected by the placement of the dark and hairy knee. Until you understand it through the flopping of the doll's head on its broken neck, or through the shaking of the camera. The shaking of the camera is really a deep, suppressed chuckle. It means different things about love every time you view it, and you've watched every night for a week, an observer of other people's domestic bliss. The little girl transforming words, her language folded into a love note to her parents. Of love becoming the dark, hairy knee. Of love represented by the cracker guts smeared into the rug.

On the tiny screen, the glow slices through your pupil until the image has embedded itself in your brain. The little girl touching the kneecap, a circular fragment that will play on indefinitely. It could shake now, it could gyrate, but it would be from a different emotional earthquake. This isn't your memory, but it could be. You have thousands that are similar. You're not sure how to dislodge them without cutting out other important parts of your brain.

Squirrels fight in the branches of the oak. Their aggressive chatter startles nearby birds from the tree; they take flight as a solitary unit. Dead leaves fall from the squirrel's nest, bits of it drifting and collecting on the sidewalk below. The tree hangs over the front of the house and blocks the sun from shining in through the picture window. You liked this tree at first sight; you claimed it kept the power bill down in the summer when the Florida sun beat mercilessly on your head and the roof of your car. Molly didn't care for it, until you'd pointed out that the base of the tree was like the palm of a giant hand, the branches spread like radiating fingers. You'd boosted her until she sat in the V, her thighs cradled in her own palms to prevent scrapes from the bark. Later there's a picture of the two of them, together, in the same position. Molly's hands were under your daughter's legs while her own were rubbed raw. That night, you kissed the red chafe marks while Molly lay facedown on the bed, pressing her laughs down into the duvet.

"I could get used to this," she'd whispered. She hadn't wanted to wake the baby.

"Do it." You'd licked a wet strip up the tender skin until the flesh shook. "Get used to it."

The baby monitor stayed silent that night and you'd been grateful. You'd thought you'd always be grateful to hear nothing but white noise from the alarm system that had woken you almost every night for over two years. That night the static had been erotic, super-charged with something that stopped your ears with cotton fuzz. At your core was a battery that powered the movement of your body. You're not sure you would have heard the baby even if you'd been listening for her. Everything was Molly and tending the ache.

You look at the monitors now and wonder if they work both ways. If they're anything like that *Twilight Zone* episode where a child receives a play telephone from his grandmother before she dies, where they have conversations through the invisible wires, beyond the grave. You press the monitor up to your ear and let your lips graze the pinholes of the audio output.

"Hello?" you say.

"Are you out there?"

There's probably someone out there, but it's another person's baby, not your daughter. Now they make monitors with inset television screens so you can watch your child sleep peacefully, and not worry for a single second that something's happening just down the hall while you kiss the slopes of your wife's breasts.

"Long Distance Call" was the name of that episode. You suddenly remember that the dead grandmother was trying to get the little boy to run out into the street. She wanted him to get hit by a car because she was lonely. You can almost understand that level of desperation.

There's room for the baby monitors at the bottom of the cardboard box labeled **GIVEAWAYS**, but you don't put them inside. You keep them in your nightstand, in case you need another reminder.

Molly's petting your stomach and you want to bite her hand. She's leaning against you on the couch with her feet up on the ottoman and reading a novel for her book club that she's already read three times. The cover is bent down the middle, and the white line that's bleeding through the words at the center demonstrates how your wife takes care of all her books—leaving them in cars and at the DMV, outside on the patio table where it'll wind up sopping wet from a summer shower. You want to turn up the volume on the television, but every time the numbers dart up past the number five she looks up with that wrinkle between her eyes that's gradually deepening into a crevasse.

"C'mon," she says. "I want to finish this tonight."

The coffee on her breath is sour but not enough to stop you from kissing her.

"I want to watch this movie." Your finger fits exactly into the groove between her eyes. She smiles and the groove flattens out, like stretching open a wrinkled shirt. You smile back. "And I'm thirsty. Can I have some orange juice?"

"Are your legs broken?" Both of you look down to where her hand still rests on your belly. The palm is flat against the curve where the minnow swims inside, still small enough to flip curlicues and roll into a ball the size of a lima bean. Her fingers twitch. "Right. I'll get it for you."

"No, it's okay."

"Sit. It's fine."

Your attempts to get up are half-hearted, and she leaves the book open with your thigh as a placeholder while she gets your drink. You weren't that thirsty; instead you spread out a little more comfortably on the sofa and turn up the volume on something you weren't even really watching. It's one of those rom-coms where the protagonist is secretly in love with her best friend, the man who plans to marry a woman who isn't right for him.

You can't understand that kind of romance. From the moment you'd met your wife, you'd met your best friend. It was at a Halloween party thrown by a guy you barely knew from your sociology class. The only reason you'd decided to go was because you couldn't stomach watching scary movies all night in your pajamas while your roommate sneakily boned her boyfriend in the bed five feet from yours.

Molly was dressed as one of the little dead girls from *The Shining*, but she was standing alone. You'd told her you liked her knee socks and asked her to say the famous line. When she did, you'd told her that your name was Danielle but that everyone called you Dani. She'd laughed and told you that her girlfriend had bailed so she'd had to wear the costume alone. You were the only one who'd known who she was supposed to be. She put her hand on your arm and you could feel the warmth of her fingertips all the way through your shirt. You'd told her she didn't feel like a dead girl. She'd smiled, revealing a crooked left canine. She'd asked if you wanted to find out for sure.

That night back in your dorm room, she'd peeled off your banana costume and made a joke about splitting after the night was over, but in the morning she was still there. She'd broken up with her girlfriend still lying on the bed beside you, whispering darkly into your telephone. Her hair was red in the light from the half-opened blinds. There were sleep creases on her cheek and you thought she was the best looking woman you'd ever seen.

Molly brings you the juice and it's in your favorite glass, the one with the etched olive leaves in green around the lip. She hands it to you and your fingers brush together and it's like you're twenty years old in a college dorm room all over again. You take a sip of the juice and it's like fire on your tongue, so sweet and pulpy that you're nearly chewing through each gulp.

"Could I have another?" you ask.

There's a beat while she stares at your belly, as if the orange juice is flowing down directly to the bulge. As if she could stand there and watch it swell further.

"Yes, of course." She kisses your sticky mouth and when she puts her hand back on your belly, you remember putting your hand on hers and feeling the life inside, struggling against the walls of the womb. This baby's calm in comparison.

They're coming to pick up the boxes from the spare room. Even though you're going to have another baby and the baby will live in that space, you don't call it the baby's room. It's just empty. There's something sickly-sweet on the back of your tongue when you think about it that way, as if you're sealing up part of your house from the rest, like it might contaminate all the other clean rooms. The walls are still powder pink and there's a large gash where you'd tried to hang the quilt your grandmother made for you when you were a toddler and the hammer went straight through the drywall.

Molly boxed up all the things one night when you were out with some work friends. When you came home, they were stacked and labeled in a handwriting you didn't recognize—severe block print in dark permanent marker: **CLOTHING, INFANT AGE 0-12 MONTHS** and then **CLOTHING, TODDLER** with no date given after the word **TODDLER**, even though you know for a fact that the clothes only go up to age three. You never had a reason to buy anything older than that—no tween clothes with glitter, or jeans, or flannel shirts, which is what you wore for all of your thirteenth year while you scowled at your own mother and cut off your hair with scissors in your best friend Becky's bathroom. She'd shaved the underside of your head and nicked you a few times. Those cuts had scabbed up bright red and while you'd slept on Becky's bed that night, your scalp had adhered to the bed sheet. When you'd woken up the next day, you'd had to peel your head away from the fabric. Your mom hadn't spoken to you for two weeks afterward. You swore you'd never be that kind of mother.

A few boxes of toys are in the pile, but you're mostly interested in the one at the top of the stack. Molly had run out of packing tape, so the box's flaps are slightly open, revealing a dark gap. There's an arm poking out from the top—a disembodied thing waving at you. You're trying to think what doll that arm could belong to, but you can't remember. You can even see a bit of its sleeve poking up along with the tanned baby flesh, flowered fuchsia and lime green.

This should be enough of a clue, but you still can't place it. You pull one of the dining room chairs over to the stack and climb on top to look inside. If Molly were home, she'd yell at you to get down and ask if you were crazy. She wouldn't ask if you were trying to kill the baby, but that's what she would think as she looked at you with her eyes all shiny and hot enough to break open and spill. You pull out the doll and it's wearing a bonnet on its fat head, covered with blonde sausage curls, gathered at each side of its rosy plastic cheeks. The eyes blink open slowly and they're green, bright green like the print on the dress. It smells moth-eaten and old, like the inside of an attic. You wonder if it was a gift from one of your great aunts. No matter how long you stare at the doll, you can't manage to place her. Was she Molly's?

The doll's lips are pink and pursed, and there as small black hole where a nipple from a tiny plastic bottle would fit. You never fed your daughter from a bottle. You heard it might cause NIPPLE CONFUSION. This was a term you whispered to each other, you and your wife, back when she was still breast feeding. It had seemed like the most awful thing you could experience. What if your daughter had NIPPLE CONFUSION and wouldn't take the breast? The doll is missing hair from the back of its head from where the strands became too brittle and broke off. You wonder if your daughter could have eaten some, that perhaps it had obstructed her airway. You know this isn't true, but you think it anyway.

When the doorbell rings, you're still standing on the chair. You don't answer the door, even though they press the bell four more times and Molly's going to get angry because the boxes are going to sit stacked in the room for another few weeks. You can't remember where you got the doll and you stand on the chair and you cry over it until you hear your wife's car in the driveway. Then you go in the bathroom and splash your face with cold water until your eyes look normal again.

The girl has a birthmark shaped like a crescent moon waxing at her right temple. It's mid-afternoon and outside the sun is high over her left shoulder. She's wearing a pair of dark jean overalls that are cutoff at the knee and a white t-shirt with the neck yanked out, as if she's been pulling at it a lot or maybe someone grabbed her. She's got a mass of dark hair floating round her head and she's wearing clear plastic jelly shoes. Her naked toes wriggle around inside them like tiny pink shrimp.

"I'm selling wrapping paper," the girl says. "They told me you might buy some."

You watch the girl's mouth seal closed again. It's small and set like fine red stitches, a ragdoll's lips that would have to be cut open with a seam ripper.

"Who's they?" you ask, though you already know who they are. The elderly neighbors next door know you're a sucker for kids. It makes them feel better for turning her away to give her another bell to ring instead.

The girl doesn't answer. The silence is oppressive, like someone's pressing a pillow against her face and slowly suffocating her.

"What's your name?" you ask, because someone has to talk now.

"Bianca."

There's a catalog hanging limply from her hand. You reach out for it and she yanks it away, like you're trying to steal it from her. "What kind of wrapping paper?"

She unfurls the catalog and you can see the sweaty imprint of her hand. You bet she must be hot, walking around all day in the Florida heat, but maybe it's weird to offer her a drink. She looks too young to be out alone, no older than eight or nine. You crane your neck, but you don't see a parent waiting down at the end of the driveway. You'd wait down at the end of the driveway, if you were her mother.

"We got all kinds. It's for school. If I sell the most, I get a bike."

Her hand touches yours as she passes you the catalog. Her fingers are sticky, like all kids hands feel. Tacky. How your daughter's hands felt when she woke up from naps covered in sweat, cranky until she got some juice and maybe some goldfish crackers or pretzels in her stomach. The girl has a sweat mustache beading over her lip.

"Let me get you a drink." You can't help yourself, though the girl's face is closing up again. "I've got some ice water?" You back up with your hands in the air. "Stay there, I'll be right back."

In the kitchen you take down a small juice glass, one of the charming relics that you got from your great grandmother that you never actually use. The light shines through it and makes patterns on the countertop. You take out every container from the fridge, cranberry and orange and pineapple and mango, but you wonder if she could have a food allergy. You decide on the ice water, just to be safe.

You crush the ice using the panel in the fridge door. You wouldn't want her to choke.

Out in the hallway, the glass cold in your palm, there's no one there. You stand holding the catalog and the drink until it starts to sweat between your fingers. Then you drink it all and close the front door before mosquitoes get inside.

At the shopping mall near your house they've got four different baby stores. You've shopped around in them before, but now you're in the biggest baby department with one of those guns that look like a phaser from Star Trek. You've made the joke *Beam me up, Scotty* so many times that your wife has stopped acknowledging you. Molly's got a list on her phone of what you need, and she's letting you shoot every item with the red dot. It scans over things like liners and diaper pails and a changing table with a pad the color of the antacids you carry in your purse because your indigestion is so bad that your throat's practically on fire.

"What about wash cloths," Molly asks, staring at the tiny screen. "Get some of those."

"We already have wash cloths."

"Not these ones, not the small ones—ours are too rough for baby skin."

You point the gun at a stack of tiny fabric squares and fire away—four, five, six times in a row.

"Take it easy, nobody needs that many." Molly puts her hand in front of the gun and you see the bright red dot on her palm. You fire at the heart of her hand and a sale price comes up for $4.99.

"Pretty cheap date," you say. She swats your behind and laughs.

Throughout the store, other mothers and grandmothers and husbands and expectant fathers load up carts with expensive equipment that their babies will only use for a few years, possibly only a few months. Babies outgrow everything so quickly. You only used that diaper disposal system for the first two months. It had cost over sixty dollars. Then you just threw the diapers away with the garbage.

There are cribs against the far wall with mobiles already attached. Some are painted pastel and others look like relics from a doomed medieval church.

"I think we'd have to name our child Tybalt if we got one of these." You point at a mobile hung with tiny realistic dragons, wings extended and jaws open. The dragons all have sharp white teeth in tiny rows like grains of uncooked rice. "Only nobility could deal with this at night."

"What about Beatrice?" Molly asks, pushing at the mobile with one fingertip until the dragons are circling the prey down below—the imagined tender, milk-fed baby for their feast. "That's a pretty name."

You think of your daughter's crib, one that had once belonged to your older sister and her two children. It's back at her house now, folded up and stacked against the wall of the closet of her guest bedroom. The wood had been the color of Molly's hair, a kind of burnt red that looked sweet with the rest of the furniture—an old rocking hair that had been Molly's mother's when she was pregnant, a toy chest that they'd found at a garage sale two streets over from their house. Molly had waddled up seven months pregnant and demanded a price reduction by half. The man selling the chest had given her the deal and then actually loaded the thing in their car.

"Maybe Sir Robin," you say, shooting at a little mobile of matchbox cars. They sway delicately in the air conditioned breeze. "I've always liked *Monty Python*."

On the back of the wrapping paper catalog, there's a name: Bianca Minarik. There's also the name of the local elementary school in your neighborhood. You decide to walk the catalog over and order a few rolls of Christmas paper, just to make up for the fact that you've kept it for over a week. It's still early enough in the day that you don't drive your car; just your keys and the catalog clutched in your fist. Only a fifteen-minute walk. You could probably use the exercise.

Overhead the sun is a hot ball of butter that's seeping salt into the corners of your eyes. You're thirsty and wish you'd thought to bring some water. It's not until you're ten minutes into your walk that you realize you've gone the wrong direction. There's a sprinkler going off in a yard across the street and you're very close to walking through it, just to cool off.

You find yourself walking up the driveway of the closest house. One foot in front of the other. When you ring the bell, you remember the episode of the crime show where the pregnant woman was abducted by someone and they cut the baby out of her stomach and kept it. You put your hand on your belly. You imagine your daughter walking up to a house and needing help. You never even got to have the stranger danger talk with her, something you'll have to do with this new child with no practice ahead of time.

The doorbell rings five times before you give up. The stretch of driveway is too long to walk back down. You sit on the front step, in the shade, and wait for you don't even know what. There's nothing to do, nothing to think. You're dizzy and feel like you might throw up. You don't even know that the door has opened behind you until you feel the cold air conditioning hit your back.

"What do you want?" The woman is elderly. She's wearing a rose chenille robe and ratty house slippers in the same pale color. The toes are ripped and dirty.

"I'm pregnant, I'm overheated. Please."

The woman keeps the door half-open and doesn't move toward you to help. The breeze from the house is intoxicating; you sway backwards into it every few seconds.

"You don't look pregnant," she says. "How do I know for sure?"

You put a hand over your belly again. How does a person know they're pregnant? When Molly was pregnant with your daughter, you knew because she peed on a stick and showed it to you over a pizza. It was a pepperoni pizza and every time afterward you ate that kind of pizza, it reminded you of how happy you were to be a mother. You were pregnant then, but you weren't pregnant, Molly was pregnant. Now that daughter is gone, and it's like no one was ever pregnant with her at all.

The sky blacks into pinpricks and then into nothing. When your eyes open again, you're laid out flat on the concrete slab of the woman's porch. She's kneeling over you with a cool cloth on your face.

Her robe is parted and you can see inside to where her nightgown gapes open to show her wrinkled breasts.

"It's okay, sweetheart." She rubs the cloth over your eyes. "Don't be scared."

It's important that you stay on the couch. Molly is working from home for the next few weeks, the bedroom set up as a home office. She's given you the remote control, a big bowl of cereal with extra milk, and the baby monitor from your nightstand. The other one is sitting next to her, in the bedroom, so she can hear you if you need to get up or if you would like more milk for your cereal after all (you always end up drinking it first).

"Now I'm watching television," you yell. "Now I'm eating my cereal."

There's nothing on that's any good. You're watching *The Price is Right*, but you miss Bob Barker and it's just not the same as when you were a kid. Back then, home from school was a good time. This feels like prison. Stuck on the couch means stuck in the house means your legs feel restless and all you want to do is go drive somewhere that's away.

Light glows red from the front of the baby monitor. That's how you know that it's on and that it's working; the evil red eye that stares out at you, that lets you know that Molly is listening to every last thing you do while she's working in the bedroom.

"Are okay out there?" she's yelling from the back, and you want to pretend like you can't hear her, but you know that's childish.

"I'm fine," you say. "Ten-Four. Over and out."

On screen a woman runs up on stage. She's wearing a bright red t-shirt that says "CINCINATTI LOVES TO COME ON DOWN." She jumps around until her shirt lifts and you can see the fishy white of her stomach.

The doorbell rings and Molly walks out from the back. "Don't get up," she says, but she's not even looking at you. She has her hair up in a high ponytail and she's wearing yoga pants even though she's never gone to a yoga class in her life. She doesn't need to; she still has the ass of a teenager.

You can hear her talking to somebody, and then there are several men in your living room, following your wife across the house. You're still in your nightgown and you don't even have time to pull the blanket up over yourself.

"Hello," you say, weakly, and one of the men smiles at you. They're all wearing matching navy polos from a local church organization.

"The boxes are over here," Molly says, and you realize that they're finally picking up your daughter's things.

They carry them out one by one across the living room in front of the show where the woman is competing to win herself a brand new car by rolling a pair of giant foam dice across a table. The guy who waved at you is carrying the box with the doll arm sticking out from the top and you can still see the little slip of lime green sleeve. You pick up the baby monitor, which is pastel pink and baby lavender and you look at the black pinholes in the face, a round mouth like a telephone. You put it to your lips.

"They're taking your stuff," you say. "I can't stop them."

Once it's all gone, the men leave and your wife comes to sit beside you on the couch. She put your legs in her lap, even though they feel still and unmovable like tree trunks.

"I love you," she says. "I love you so much."

"I love you too," you reply. Then you whisper it into the baby monitor, to whoever might be listening.

lebkuchen

Anja Dieter had skin that glowed like a fluorescent light bulb and hands that felt like crumpled tissue paper. People in the neighborhood guessed that she was aged anywhere from thirty to forty-five, because she possessed a densely square figure that had probably looked middle-aged since puberty. Her arms and legs were nearly the same length, and she wore dresses in a variety of bright, geometric patterns to compensate for her innate squatness. Though her face was slightly pugnacious with its flat, upturned nose, there was a doughy sweetness to it: pink rounded cheeks, dark eyes like thumb-pressed raisins, her mouth a wide wet knife slash of red gums and square chicklet teeth.

The Dieters lived on the cusp of the neighborhood's only cul-de-sac. Their boxy beige ranch was an unwanted party guest sat down next to a half-circle of sherbet colored dream houses, beautiful homes with juicy green lawns thanks to intricate sprinkler systems. The Dieter's yard was crisp and full of sandspurs. The neighborhood kids knew better than to run barefoot through their grass.

Nina Braithwaite lived along the same scallop of homes. She kept her waist trim through vigorous aerobic activity and juice cleanse recipes collected from *Redbook* and *Woman's Day* magazine. She lived with her husband in a big white colonial with a King Charles Spaniel called Dexter that she'd named after her grandfather, and a daughter called Madison who had been named after a popular street in New York City.

Though Nina had been the Dieter's neighbor for over six years, she knew almost nothing about Anja or her family. They didn't socialize with the rest of the neighbors—no backyard barbeques or invitations to birthday parties. The patriarch was a dinosaur of mysterious background, a Colonel Randolph Dieter, whom everyone had always called the Colonel, though nobody knew why because he'd never served in the army.

"The Colonel is suffering from hemorrhoids again." Nina overheard Anja say to Judy Clarkson while delivering some misdirected mail. "He must remember to sit on his inflatable doughnut."

The Colonel was very old. He walked rigidly upright, as if fitted with a brace, and he always wore a dark suit and a black derby hat. Nina sometimes saw him eating at a Turkish restaurant downtown that served extremely bitter coffee.

Nina knew even less about Anja's mother. Rosa Dieter had passed away some seven years prior. Current speculation in the neighborhood was that Rosa had been a practicing Wiccan. The basis for this rumor was that Bonnie Smithwick had claimed to see a tarot deck in the backseat of the Dieter's station wagon, and that Rosa had planted an herb garden by her mailbox. The neighborhood association had sent a cease and desist letter telling her that the garden was in violation of the mandated landscaping—boxed hedges must be placed below windows, trees planted with ten-foot spacing, absolutely no edible plants.

Someone had spray painted "Anja Dieter Is A Fucking Cyborg" on the side of a building downtown. It stayed up for over a month. Nina stared at it every time she went to go pick up the dry cleaning. Paint dripped lewdly from each letter, a small boxy shape drawn below it that could have been a robot or crudely drawn genitals. Nina thought Anja's face was less robotic and more like a slick mask. She'd never heard the woman laugh or seen her smile, except at the young children she babysat. She never took visitors and she never went on trips; no one had ever seen her operate a car. Anja Dieter walked back and forth across the same swath of asphalt day in and day out. She babysat for nearly every family in the neighborhood.

"She's harmless," Bonnie Smithwick said when Anja had shown up to babysit wearing a full-length freezer coat in the middle of summer. "Just modest. I think she might be religious."

The children all liked her because she told bedtime stories where the characters sometimes died at the end. She killed indiscriminately. Some nights the heroes survived their ordeals intact, victorious over some dire situation in which they might race a speeding train, or rescue an entire apartment building going down in flames. Other nights they might get eaten by wild dogs, the heroes chewed to splintered fragments.

On an afternoon in early July, Anja Dieter walked in on Nina Braithwaite and Bonnie Smithwick in the Braithwaite's master bedroom suite. The two women caught the movement in the doorway and threw themselves off the mattress. Bonnie yanked an overlarge pillow off the bed to cover herself. The pink satin case hung half off, dangling down around her knees like a filmy skirt. Nina pulled an afghan off the back of an overstuffed chintz reading chair and wrapped it around her body and tucked the end up under her arms like a bath towel.

"Mrs. Braithwaite," Anja said. "Your daughter was playing outside alone. I gave her a popsicle from the truck."

The smooth blandness of Anja's face could have meant that she was meeting two casual acquaintances at the frozen food aisle of the grocery store. She stood in the doorway and wiped her palms against her dress.

"The twins are in the kitchen having popsicles too, Mrs. Smithwick." Anja had been watching Bonnie's kids next door. "I think the air conditioner is broken at your house."

A hideous, braying sob ripped from Bonnie Smithwick. She dropped the silk pillow to cover her mouth in a belated attempt to retract the noise. Her bare breasts were tiger striped from the incoming slats of sunshine through the vertical blinds.

"We'll be just a minute." Nina's smile was a tight grit of overly white teeth.

Once the door was closed, there was an explosion of activity. A search for clothing, hissed whispers and accusations.

"Why didn't you lock the door?"

"My daughter's home, remember?"

"Why is she here, what is she *doing here?*" Bonnie Smithwick's voice rose to a quivering shriek. Nina flapped her hands at her impatiently and then pulled on her pants. They were linen and wrinkled from being on the floor.

"I don't know. I don't know."

They dressed hastily. When they emerged from the room their walk was stilted, as if they didn't know what to do with their limbs. Bonnie compulsively smoothed down the back of her hair, which was frizzy and prone to cowlicks. The children were already in the living room watching a movie on the flat-screen television. The previews before the feature presentation were full of loud sound effects of explosions. Nina asked if the two women would like a light lunch.

"Turkey wraps? I've got a recipe that uses organic avocado, it really is fabulous."

They clumped around the glass topped kitchen table, a summer salad bowl central to the radiating arms of gilded fruit plates and long-stemmed crystal drinking goblets. Nina had put out the cloth napkins. Bonnie chattered nervously about the freshness of the avocado, gesturing at it with her fork until a bit flew off and landed on her skirt. When she finally stopped talking her face settled down into a thin-lipped grimace. Nina patted her lips with her napkin even though she hadn't taken a single bite of food.

"How do you like it, Anja?"

"It's weird." Anja took three consecutive sips of the tea, which she'd sweetened with half a plastic bottle of honey. "I don't like it very much."

Nina set her napkin down on the table and made Anja a peanut butter and jam sandwich. Anja didn't say thank you. She chewed her food very slowly, like an elderly person. Her jaws opened and shut carefully, as if considering how her teeth and gums would land on each chunk of peanut. It was very quiet in the room aside from the sounds of chewing and the occasional rapid-fire burst of the laugh track from the other room. Bonnie ignored Anja entirely. Her feet shifted restlessly underneath the table until it became counterpoint to the chewing, a light hiss from her flats scuffing across the tile.

When she was finished eating, Anja took her napkin and unfolded it flat over the dissected chunks of food still on her plate.

"Mrs. Smithwick, I'd still like to get paid."

Bonnie's expression was brittle. Her eyes had a glassy look to them from the couple of Xanax she'd popped in the bathroom before the meal. Nina thought she looked half asleep.

"What? Of course I'll pay you, I always pay you, right?" Her hands fumbled around as she looked beneath the table for her purse. "Although I'm not sure why, you only watched them for half an hour."

When she sat up again she smiled and there was a sliver of lettuce covering one of her front teeth. She reached out and grabbed both of Anja's hands, which were still sitting on top of her crumpled napkin.

"You aren't going to say anything to anyone about this, are you?"

"What would I say?" Anja asked.

"I think we're done here," Nina said. "Unless anyone's still hungry?"

Bonnie stood up awkwardly and the movement brought her chair scraping backwards against the ceramic tile.

"I've got to be going. Tyler is bringing over some clients tonight, I have to start the roast." She walked out of the kitchen to collect her kids without saying goodbye. Her purse was left hanging on the back of her chair.

"I want another sandwich, Mrs. Braithwaite."

Nina got up and made two more with extra jam. She handed one to Anja and ate the other sandwich herself, elbows on the table, staring hard at her lunch guest. Anja drank the last of the tea and then dug out the honey-covered ice cubes with her fingers. She crunched on the cubes and the noise was loud like sudden bursts of radio static.

That night while she was brushing her hair in the bathroom, Nina asked her husband what he thought of Anja Dieter.

"I don't think anything about her. She watches our kid." He stopped in the middle of taking off his work slacks, one foot in a black dress sock stuck out to the side like playing the hokey pokey. The hair high on his leg was thick and dark against the milky-blue skin of his inner thigh. "Did something happen with Maddie?"

Nina pulled a silk camisole over her head and stared at herself in the mirror. She turned left and then right, patting a hand over the tiny bulge of water weight she always got right before her period. "No, of course not."

"Then why'd you ask?" He poked his head in the bathroom to look at her in the mirror. The overhead lights haloed the oily spot at the crown where his hair had begun to thin.

"I don't know. Forget it." Nina pulled the brush slowly through her hair, a shiny black wave across her shoulder, floating halfway down her back. She shifted slightly and it whisked across her neck like fingertips. Her collarbone peeked through like a glimpse of white bone.

Kenneth began talking about a real estate deal at work. She tuned out in her familiar way, nodding her head, walking over to the closet to pick out her running clothes for the next morning. She put together a grocery list in her head: eggs, milk, more crunchy peanut butter.

In the past her eyes had slid over Anja's round body like the slick objects she kept around her home; a thing she'd seen so many times it had ceased to have meaning. But when Anja had walked in on her today with Bonnie, Nina had felt all of her bodily imperfections as if they were lit up by neon signs: the slight sag in her left breast, the shiny white scar across her torso from her C-section. Even the round mole that played just below her navel had suddenly felt huge and cancerous.

"Honey, does this tie match this shirt?"

"Try the blue paisley."

Anja's lack of recognition had struck something deeply discordant in Nina. It reminded her of her freshman year in college when she'd gained thirty pounds her first semester away from home. Only a year, but it felt like longer. She'd missed her mother's cooking, and she'd felt out of her depth, lost and floating in a sea of girls who'd looked just like her. She'd consoled herself with tubs of frosting, loved herself with brownie batter, and had melted endless sticks of butter mixed with white sugar to pour over crunchy toast. Her weight had ballooned and she'd been miserable and confused, unsure how to move in a body so foreign and unnatural feeling. Her limbs were puffy and her face was a soft marshmallow. Her stomach rumbled thinking about it.

In the mirror, Nina's eyes were hugely dilated. She went into the bedroom and crawled on top of her husband, who was reading one of the pulpy spy paperbacks he favored. His rimless half-moon glasses pressed down into his jowly cheeks. Nina clutched his hands when he would have shut off the bedside light—so she could watch his eyes watch her, so she could see herself reflected back as she rose and fell on top of him. She thought of Anja Dieter and closed her eyes; her stomach bottomed out and her thighs trembled.

Nina had shown up at the Dieter's house two days later carrying an arrangement of fresh flowers from her back garden. The bouquet was heavy on gardenia and the smell clung to her face and hands. Anja answered the door in a blue-checked smock. She showed no confusion or upset, but neither did she show any pleasure.

"I thought you might enjoy a visitor?"

"You are not a visitor, you are my employer."

Nina tried not to be offended. She held the flowers in front of her body as a shield, unsure if she should walk back down the path that led to the street and go back home. She wondered if she should make some small talk about the weather. It was hot outside and the petals of the flowers were drooping. Her armpits had begun to perspire and she worried it might be seen through the thin fabric of her dress.

Anja stepped backward and motioned her inside. The rooms were painted a pale, sticky pink and the hallway that led to the living area felt cramped with a very low ceiling. The walls were covered in family portraiture that seemed too old; sepia photography where the faces looked angry. The wood floors were impossibly slick. At one point Nina had to place her hand against the wall to steady herself. Her fingers came away tacky. She rubbed them against her skirt and felt the fabric pill up.

"I was cleaning the floors." Anja was holding a can of lemon Pledge in one hand and a scrap of t-shirt in the other.

"You wax your floors with Pledge? It says not to do that right on the side of the can!"

"Who knows what's true," Anja replied. "Advertisers often lie. I've found that many products often serve more than one purpose."

In the living room, the two women sat as bookends on the uncomfortable sofa. Nina clutched the flowers to her chest and Anja held her rag. The can she sat beside her on a small side table cluttered with old *TV Guides*. Nina couldn't spot a television set anywhere.

Colonel Dieter entered the room from an adjacent hallway, wearing a white undershirt and unbuttoned black slacks with his hat. Anja got to her feet and so did Nina, though the Colonel did not acknowledge either of them. He walked into the kitchen and the women trailed along after him.

In contrast to the darkness of the house, the kitchen was airy and bright. The Colonel sat at a high formica counter and began to eat his lunch, a blue plate of white rice and boiled chicken. The gardenias that Nina had long since crushed to bits against her chest were emitting a cloying fragrance that made her feel lightheaded and sick to her stomach. Anja took them from her and filled her empty hands with a plate. Nina's heart began to thump like a rolling log. She stared at the food and stood in the middle of the kitchen with her feet splayed outward like a ballerina. Nina took the smallest bite of rice and then another, and another, until she had finished up the plate entirely.

Anja took the plate and wiped a smear of chicken grease from the corner of Nina's lip with the edge of her thumb. Nina heard waves crashing in her ears; the floor rocked under her feet. She watched Anja cleaned the dishes at the wide sink, her thick calves appearing and disappearing beneath her skirt as she stooped to place a clean bowl into a bottom cabinet. The curve of Anja's cheek seemed soft and downy as she brushed back a stripe of hair. The shine on her lips as she set them with her tongue made Nina's breath bottle up in her chest. She looked at all these small things in Anja and wanted them immediately all for herself. She tried to keep the look of hunger off her face.

"Your daughter is a wonderful cook," Nina said.

"She isn't my daughter." He scraped the food on his plate into a pile.

Anja made no change of expression over this statement, as if she had probably heard it mentioned thousands of times over the span of her life—this old man with his worn black hat eating the food that she prepared for him day after day, discussing her life as if she were an unwanted guest in her own home.

"Is she your stepdaughter?" Nina asked.

"She's adopted. I don't know who she belongs to." He rose from the counter like a paper figure unfolding and left the room.

Anja let the comments sit heavy in the air between them. Nina wanted to touch her throat and feel where the words would come out, stroke the vocal chords and tap out the hidden messages like Morse code.

"Did you want something else?" Anja asked. She turned back to the stack of dishes.

"Not right now," Nina replied.

It was quiet in the house except for a bird singing outside the kitchen window and the noise of a car pulling into a nearby driveway. Nina excused herself and walked out.

For the next few weeks, Nina Braithwaite trailed Anja around the neighborhood. She took her morning runs later and later in the day, watching for when Anja would be walking the cul-de-sac to her next babysitting appointment. She'd run past and Anja would ignore her—would look directly over her head at the cloudless expanse of sky.

Nina dropped out of her social clubs one by one; she spent less time fixing up her home and more time trying to suss out information on Anja Dieter, coaxing morsels and gleaning bits from her daughter with bribes of pizza and soda.

"Anja doesn't like anything," Maddie had said. "Maybe candy."

Judy Clarkson told her that Anja preferred the color green, so she took to draping herself in swaths of it—rich shades that made her skin look like ivory.

"They have that same material on sale at fabric store; it looks itchy." Anja said about a leaf green paisley print crepe dress that had cost four hundred dollars. Nina cut it up with scissors when she got home, let Maddie keep bits of the material for her dolls to wear.

Nina found ways to be home on Friday night, but still pay Anja to babysit—claiming a headache in the middle of dinner, or an upset stomach just when the movie was about to start at the theater. She would ask to drive Anja home. She began obsessively eating chicken and rice, boiling it in her kitchen just so she could smell the warm food. The scent of stock clung to her clothes and hair.

Bonnie Smithwick began tentatively calling again, and when she got no response, took to dropping by the house for playdates with the kids. When she realized that all Nina wanted to talk about was Anja Dieter, she was incredulous.

"Maybe I'll stop by and see if Anja can make me a meal," Bonnie said, laughing as she ran her fingers along the edge of the iced tea glass.

Nina ignored her, but on her next run she saw Bonnie coming out of the Dieter house with a wrapped plate of chicken, and Nina felt her blood boil beneath the skin. Her own husband began talking about Anja in a way that made Nina look at him from the corner of her eye.

"That Dieter girl has filled out pretty nicely, huh?"

"What's that supposed to mean, Kenneth?"

"You could stand to gain a few pounds, that's all." He'd smiled, poking playfully at her side. It was a finger nudge meant to be gentle, but it felt as though she'd been speared.

Her body pulled inward as cadaverously as Anja Dieter's had blossomed outward. Nina was ravenous. She snuck spoonfuls of Nutella, smearing it on cookies between her runs. She made layer cakes and devoured them all herself in the middle of the night with giant glasses of chocolate milk, but her ribs still poked through her skin until she could nestle her fingers between them.

One night she'd come home from picking up Kenneth's dry cleaning and saw him leaning up against the mailbox out front, the one they'd bought to look like a mini replica of their own house. He'd been watching the kids play down the street in front of the Clarkson's and rubbing at the back of his neck where his hair was starting to get a little shaggy over his shirt collar. Anja Dieter was kneeling in the front yard pulling weeds in a large plum housecoat and rain boots. Her rump was in the air, resembling a large purple heart. Nina wanted to shield her with the dry cleaning bags.

The Dieters were suddenly invited to all of the dinners. There were potlucks to which Anja brought the Colonel and platters of boiled chicken, cookouts at the Hallford's with Anja and the Colonel sitting uncomfortably to the side while the women sipped sangria and the men grilled steaks and drank cases of local beer. Cocktails at sundown with Anja glowing waxy-white, the Colonel stoic at her side while he sweltered in his best suit.

At a wine and cheese mixer at the Clarkson's house, a sprawling Victorian brimming with cats and potted ferns, Anja had spoken only a handful of words though people had approached her from all sides. Nina sat nearby and watched Anja's mouth move, tried to determine minute facial expressions to see what could possibly show her favor and her distaste, a way to know how she felt so she could coax those feelings for herself.

"Would you like some more wine?" Judy asked Anja, holding up a perfectly chilled bottle of white.

Anja's glass was still full to the brim. "Why would I want more?"

"Is there something wrong with it?" Judy touched Anja's forearm, just a glance of fingers, but Nina's insides clenched.

"It's not good." Anja held out her glass. "It curdles my stomach."

Anja went into the kitchen of the big house alone. Nina followed her, told her husband that she needed to use the restroom. She watched Anja rifle through cabinets, pulling out milk—condensed and fresh, and some sugar. She mixed these together in a plastic cup and drank it down. Not in quick gulps, but slow sips that made her throat move rhythmically above her high collar. When she put down the glass, she had a fat white mustache curling above her lip.

"It hurts," Anja said, holding her belly.

Nina stepped forward and placed her hands on either side of Anja's torso without touching her, her hands hovering and fluttering as if taking a psychic reading. The heat came off her skin in waves.

She poured Anja another glass of milk and added bourbon with the sugar, mixed it up with her finger. Anja drank it and then laid her head on Nina's shoulder. They sat in the kitchen like that for another ten minutes, listening to the sounds of the party going on in the opposite room.

It was a Monday morning with the skies partly cloudy with a twenty percent chance of rain. Anja sat on the floor with Maddie showing the girl how to build shiny fish from leftover aluminum foil. Nina sat on the couch and watched them. She drank glass after glass of water. Her stomach felt hollow.

"Crimp it with your whole hand—yes, like that."

Anja took the fish and strung it with the others on fishing line, then hung them all in the back window overlooking the swimming pool. They swayed listlessly in the glass, their google eyes staring out into the summer humidity.

"More?" Maddie asked.

"Not now," Nina said. "I want Anja to help me make the beds."

The beds in the house were all large and Nina hated to make them by herself, would have given them all over to Anja if she could, but Anja was not their maid and Nina liked to watch the swift, precise movements of Anja's arms as she tucked the sheets and fluffed up pillows.

In the master bedroom they stood on opposite sides of the bed. The fitted sheet sailed white over their heads as they fluffed it up and down together as a parachute, until it finally settled into the corners of the mattress. As Nina came around to grab the stack of leftover linens, Anja reached for the quilt. Their bodies met and pressed. Nina kissed Anja's eyebrows, her full cheeks, and the line down her throat. She held onto her waist, the firmness of her hips dense beneath her fingers.

Nina thought that squeezing Anja's flesh wasn't exactly like kneading dough, but that it was similar. There was a lump of heavy breast, and then there was the heavy wrap of her stomach. The ripeness Nina was grabbing had as much significance as tearing into a piece of bread. She had to stop herself from digging her nails into the soft curve of the woman's hip.

And while it happened, Nina waited to finally feel fulfilled, but Anja was silent and made no sound as she was devoured in small, precise bites. When it was over, they lay tangled in the half-drawn sheets. Anja clung to Nina's waist and Nina's hands didn't know where to set on Anja's skin. She remembered a different day, with a different woman in the same set of sheets and couldn't tell their bodies apart. There was a bitter taste in Nina's mouth like the inside of an apple core. The room was humid and smelled of musk; she worried that the seeping fragrance of Anja's yeasty body would become Nina's scent— that Braithwaite would become Dieter; that she wouldn't be able to leave behind the body that she had ingested.

Nina dressed herself and left the house without saying anything to Anja. She walked to the park down the street and sat out on a bench by the shore of the lake. An elderly woman was looking after a small girl with messy blonde hair, handing her fat slices of bread to feed the ducks. It began to rain and the little girl threw the rest of the bread on the ground and covered her head with her arms. The older woman scooped up the girl and jogged to a nearby car. They drove away while Nina sat and let her clothes soak up the wet.

The ducks were gorging themselves on the leftover bread. One of the smaller birds was choking on a very large piece. Its sleek body jerked back and forth as it worked to swallow the fattest part of the dough. Nina gagged and turned away, then gagged some more until she finally threw up in a nearby garbage can. When she was done, she wiped her lips with the hem of her shirt. Her stomach felt empty and light. She decided to walk back down the street to Bonnie's house so she could use her bathroom to wash her face and hands, maybe take a bath in the big claw foot tub. The rain on the asphalt made her footsteps sound like slaps.

The Dieter's beige house seemed dark in the rain, a dank murky brown. Her eyes slid over it and caught on Bonnie's house with its big red door and porch full of tall white columns. She wondered if Bonnie might let her take a nap on her couch. Nobody answered the front door, so she went around the back of the house and unlatched the wooden gate. The pool was under a covered patio and was heated year-round by a solar panel up on the roof. Nina stepped in with all of her clothes on. The warm water crept up her legs and stomach and neck, and when her feet could no longer reach the bottom, she let herself drift and sink.

A Decline in Natural Numbers

5.

Working backwards from the ends, Brianna rolls her hair in a twist without looking at a mirror. It takes one long pin to pierce it, stabbing down until the rubber tip scrapes against her scalp. In the past, it was always done without much thought. Her mind had focused on what came after: queuing the music, relaxing her limbs into pretzels shapes on the floor, the feel of the slick wood under her fingertips. Now when she twists the knot, the hair pulls too tight or too loose, slippery like dishwater. Her hands don't remember how to shape it. Instead they crawl slowly, a foreignness that makes the roots of her hair itch. Brianna looks at her reflection over the barre to see where the hairline shows crooked. Too much on the right side means she has to shift everything over to the left, like a fifty-year-old man working at his comb over. She gets a headache from yanking at her hair, over and over, some of it coming out in her hands when she gets frustrated and pulls too hard. It's not like before, where pain at practice meant muscle memory and the ache was a familiar outcome of hard work. That was a pain that inevitably led to sweat; a long line of it that began at the center of her back and radiated outward, blossoming stains on her leotards.

Pain means something different now. Brianna stumbles over simple movements she'd learned in primary when her limbs were still doughy and pliable. There's agony in rolled ankles and pinched nerves in her neck from improper turns. She falls again and again into graceless heaps, struggling with rudimentary positions and steps until she gives herself migraines from trying to remember how her muscles should work. When she folds over to stretch her back and legs, her vision darkens into pinholes like punched tin. Lifting upward again, her head is a balloon that floats gently toward the ceiling. Her warm ups are punctuated by these gravitational shifts, swinging between the weight of memory and the lightness of unremembered space. Swooning from the altitude shifts, her damp breath kisses the mirror when she presses her face against it, trying to regain balance.

Brianna can conjure memories of how it all used to work. The oiled mechanics of her limbs, undulating, performing like a greased engine, one lubricated by sweat and practice, coiled muscles bunched up under the skin, ready to move. Dance was a place she went to get outside of her head, but now it feels as if the two have severed ties. Lifting her right leg, pivoting her left, then smoothing back her arms until they're churning the air at her sides like fluttering wings. This is from a routine that she's been practicing for weeks, but she can't remember what comes next, as if a gray partition has been put up in her brain.

adagio, slow unfolding, control

At eleven in the morning, the five year olds arrive. Babies with grown up hair, except their arms are pudding and their round bellies are full of sugary breakfast. *Sweet girls*, thinks Brianna, who used to leave the building once the youngest class started warm ups, but now she stays and sits in the corner before the instructor arrives. She watches their arms quiver above their heads. Fingers interlocked, knees visibly dimpling below their tights. How the girls all sway, side-to-side, even before the music starts. Their bodies are primed for movement. This is an introductory class, but all young female bodies must begin alignment here with their tendons like rubber bands and their muscles like cream ready to be whipped.

These girls have no breasts and some of them never will. One girl with dark eyes has good feet and she's already turned out. Brianna wants to tell her what the future looks like: a big wooden floor that happily comes up to greet you—sometimes with a smile and sometimes with a slap.

4.

"Do you ever worry that your brain has rough patches?"

Brianna's younger brother sits on the floor with a deck of cards. He's stacking them in piles of four, each topped with a different queen. They have faces like royalty inbred for five generations. He doesn't answer her, so she asks again. He sets down his cards, but he doesn't look at her.

"What do you mean, like a golf course?"

"No." She sits across from him on the rug and scoops up all the cards. Then she cuts the deck, taking half. "Not like that. Like god was sanding it down before you were born, but maybe he got busy and missed some parts."

"That doesn't make any sense."

"Sure it does." She fans out the cards. Some of them face out. "Maybe you don't notice those parts until you're older, because you don't need them right away, but then they're too craggy to use."

Jack, two, five. A card with a man on the front but she can't remember what he's called. The crown man with the sash and scepter. His profile looks wise.

"Your brain wrinkles when you learn something new—it forms ridges. A smooth brain is a baby brain, Anna."

There are two children in the Crimm family and their names both start with Brian. Brianna is older, but she didn't choose the nicknames. Brian calls her Anna and she calls him Brian—never Bri, like his friends call him when they come over to play video games and eat all the food in the freezer. Their parents collectively call them BC, which they say stands for Before Curfew, because before they had the kids they could leave the house on a Friday night.

Brianna loves her brother indulgently, like she would a grumpy housecat. He's fourteen but she remembers holding him when he was a baby. His fingers were warm and sticky and she had dressed him in doll clothes, feeding him spoonfuls of clumped rice cereal from a small yellow bowl.

"A smooth brain would be pretty like a pink bowling ball." He shakes his head at this, but she continues. "Beautifully curved."

Brianna stretches out her legs on either side of her until she is flexing the rotator cuffs in her pelvis and pointing her toes. She's missed practice all week because she's been at different doctors appointments with people poking at her, trying to figure out what's wrong with her head. In order to make it to school, the appointments are scheduled for very early in the morning. They get up before the sun, her mother piloting the car down darkened streets while the moon still hides behind the branches of the trees. It's fall break now, so she doesn't have to worry about school for a little while, which has just been making her tired. Her mother bought her reading glasses from the rack at the drug store when she picked up Brianna's latest prescription. They make the letters swim across the overhead and give her headaches.

"You don't know what you're talking about," Brian says, taking the cards from her hands. "This is boring. Let's play war."

He shuffles the deck. His fingers are thick and short and dark hair is starting to curl right above the knuckle. When he gives her half the cards, she cradles them in her lap and waits. He flips his first card so she flips hers, laying them side-by-side on the floor between their bodies. He has a three and she has a seven. One is red and one is black; there are hearts in the corners of one and the other has dark flower shapes. She doesn't take them right away, so he pushes them across the rug toward her. She picks them up and holds them until he takes them away again and sets them in a small pile next to one of her legs. The next time they flip their cards, they simultaneously reveal a pair of threes.

"What happens now?" she asks. "Now what?"

3.

In the tube there are white lights, blinking softly like Christmastime. The sides curve upward, bright and smooth, but she's not supposed to move her head to look at them. Brianna wears a paper gown, short like when she'd danced the part of Giselle last spring. When she moves her legs, the paper crinkles and in her ears it's like she's unwrapping a gift, over and over again.

"Ten more minutes. Try to remain still, please."

The woman operating the machine had already explained what would happen while Brianna sat on the table with her hands in her lap. She must lie face-up in the tube, perfectly still, while the white lights spin around her head. A round circle slowly haloes the patterns of her brain. Then the picture will be sent to the neurologist, who will talk with Brianna's mother in private, like she has been on the phone for the past few months. Brianna is always the last to know.

Giselle died of a weak heart, but Brianna's beats timpani-loud in her chest with a strong and steady rhythm.

Last week Brianna's father and mother had talked with her about staying home from school. *Just for a little while,* they'd said, and maybe Brianna's mother could show her a few things from her textbooks. *Just rest and relax your brain,* her mother had said, but Brianna's brain already felt too relaxed. The kind of relaxed that came from sleeping in late and drinking bottles of cold medicine and watching daytime television, the kind of relaxed that can't wake back up again on its own. At home, she's alone and there's no one to talk to except her mother, who sounds too bright and too sharp, and her father comes home tired and aggravated. Brian is at school during the day, and then he has soccer practice, and when he comes back inside at early evening he smells like sweat and grass and like he's been around other people. The smell of the outdoors is enough to make Brianna cry.

"Please, you have to stay still."

In class she'd been raising her hand but forgetting the question. Or she would forget the words for the questions: *who, what when, where why how* all written down in even letters on the tops of her notes. Or she would be talking to a group of friends at lunch and suddenly look at the moon of someone's face and forget who they were or how she knew them, like she'd been dropped from a great height into an unfamiliar scene, and she would get scared and hyperventilate, and then someone would call her mother.

Brianna, her mother would say in the car in the parking lot with the heat turned up so that it burned her face, *we have got to stop meeting like this.*

Brian was at her school, in the ninth grade, and sometimes in the sea of faces his would swim into focus and the sudden clarity of it was shocking—like someone had dumped a bucket of cold water over her head. She would follow him down corridors and into rooms where he sat with other boys his age who knew her name, and she would say *Brian, Brian* and he would say *Go back to class, Anna, please go back to class.*

"You're doing so great, baby, just five more minutes."

How could she tell her mother that there were days when her face looked like a mask? That Maggie Crimm, a mother who'd spent thirty-three hours in labor with her firstborn child, was sometimes a stranger to her when she walked into a room? The other morning, Brianna had gone downstairs to get breakfast and the lady behind the fat granite island in the middle of the kitchen had smiled at her. Brianna had thought *who is that woman, did we hire a maid* and she'd stood there in the doorway, waiting for an introduction, until the woman had asked *what kind of eggs do you want this morning, sweetheart?* Then the woman had turned into her mother and it had scared her so badly she'd started laughing. Her mother had laughed, too, until they were both laughing in the middle of the kitchen and neither one of them were really laughing, and actually it sounded a lot like crying.

There was a hissing in the tube like a balloon slowly deflating. The lights circled Brianna's head and she counted them in sets of five until she couldn't remember the numbers after forty.

"Just one more minute."

All the lights dimmed at once and the machine powered down. Brianna was helped to a sitting position by a woman with graying brown hair and small, cool hands who was her mother—mother-voice that tried to sound bright all the time even when it was really sad, which sometimes made it even more unbearable. She rubbed her palms in circles against her tissue paper dress and felt the crinkle in her thighs, which were still strong and muscular. Then she asked when they were going to get started; she was going to be late for dance practice.

2.

Every time rain drips on the windshield, the wipers come up to smear them back down to the bottom of the glass. The water pools there and Brianna looks at it and it magnifies the colors of the outside world: brown and green and another color that she can't remember the name of, but it looks like how the sky looks when it's wet, it's the color of nighttime creeping in before bedtime on school nights when you're not ready for your eyes to close, it's the color of the rat animals from the park that like to eat nuts from the things with the leaves.

"Are you hungry? We could pick something up."

Her mother speaks, her mother with short hair, but it used to be long like the picture that Brianna carries with her so she can remember the specifics: M O T H E R it says in black pen, M O T H E R with long hair and a big nose and space between the things in her mouth that chew food.

"Bread with the brown meat that makes it wet." Brianna breathes on the window. Wet bubbles up and she uses her finger to make a shape like two snakes kissing. "The yellow sauce and red."

"Hamburgers, got it."

Now Brianna makes forgotten words longer by turning them into sentences. Sometimes she remembers the words this way, or sometimes she still forgets them, but making the long sentences takes time and her tongue flaps around in the cave space and it makes her want to think them instead of say them, so Brianna talks less than she ever did before. M O T H E R says *where is my little chatterbox, where has she gone, where is the girl who used to talk with her dolls and her stuffed animals all night in bed, the one who would play hide and seek with her daddy but could never stay hidden because she loved to shout where she was? Is she hiding in your throat? Where is that little girl, will she ever come out again?* M O T H E R with the wet in her eyes and then wet on the pink face, wet like when the rain falls on the windshield and the wipers swoop in like rubbing hands to scrub it off again.

In the car they sit in front of the big plastic pictures of the meat and the bread and the sound comes out of the metal plate that asks if they would like to supersize anything. Brianna's mother drives the car and gives the money for the paper sack that Brianna holds on her lap like a warm puppy. It smells like the holiday with the grill that her father loves to use outside, the wet coming out of the long green rubber onto the long yellow rubber that the kids throw themselves down, and then it is nighttime and the flashes pop open in the sky like bright flowers.

"Fourth of July," says Brianna. "July the Fourth."

"Let's get home, I bet your father and brother are hungry."

M O T H E R puts the wet bread and meat on the glass circles and Brianna has a purple fruit to drink. Brian sits across from her and she tries to kick him under the table but he is looking down at the bread and the meat and his mouth is moving fast to get the food inside, big gulps of purple fruit so he can leave the empty glass circle and go upstairs to the colored screen to talk to friends. Not many people come over to their house now, not since Brianna stopped dance and not since Brianna stopped school, and not since M O T H E R quit work and stayed home so Brianna would never be alone again after she put the bread and the cheese on the red coils and did not remember to use the round metal pan.

Here is where the man shows Brianna the flashcards, after the dinner, M O T H E R has cleared the long wood and taken the glass circles to the big tub with the wet and the soap. The cards have pictures on them and Brianna must give up the words, and if she gives up the words that go with the cards, then Brianna can watch her dance videos for one hour after dinner.

"What's this called?" The man lays the card flat on the table and points at it. "We know this one."

The man says "we" when they look at the cards, but he really means Brianna, because he already knows the answer and he won't tell her what it is. He will point at the card and make his face get very pinched and say *c'mon we know this one, we know this, we looked at it yesterday, Brianna, why can't you remember this one? If you got it yesterday, then you should be able to get it today, right? So what's this word? I'll give you a hint—it's one of your favorite foods and it starts with the same letter as your name: Brianna, B for*

Brianna, so that means that it starts with a B for beautiful, just like you! Can't you tell me this word, beautiful Brianna?

"Yummy yellow smile." Brianna rubs the card. "Eat it and your stomach is happy."

"No, this is called a banana. B A NA NA."

"BAN AN A."

Cards cover the table in slick piles and M O T H E R comes and pets Brianna's head while she looks at them and tries to remember the words. The man still wants to look at them and remember the words even though Brianna says no and M O T H E R says *okay, Mike, I think that's enough for one night, don't you? Look at her—she's tired, she can't do this anymore right now* and then the man says *goddamnit, Maggie, why can't you just let her try?*

Up the stairs, climbing on sticks that the card called L E G S and Brianna's feet are tired. When she walks past the door to Brian's room, the light from the box shines through the cracks and onto the carpet. Brianna opens the door and Brian is in the bed with the lights off but the sound overhead is a clack-clack-clack; that means there's a breeze with Brian and there's no clack-clack in Brianna's room. She crawls onto the bed with Brian and he moves over so they both can hide under the nest of soft and pillow and blanket. They lay together and

Brian's face has the wet. When Brianna touches his eye he tells her to go to sleep.

1.

Maggie Crimm has one daughter and one son, but everyone knows which one she's always preferred. In the warm cocoon of the ballet studio, Maggie can tell herself truthfully that she's always loved the long swing of her daughter's hair, that she always smiled brightest when her daughter was looking out for her after school in the car line for pick up, that she maybe hugged her daughter a little harder when she would put her children to bed at night.

G I R L, what the flashcards call her daughter, long hair and soft pink dresses and a pretty way with walking and talking. What Maggie always wished she'd been like as a young girl was her own baby, petal-perfect and sweet, but Maggie had been too tall and gangly, and her mouth had been full of crooked teeth. There was a wide gap between the front two that felt sloppy, what her own mother had said looked *loose and easy,* and it made her want to smile with her mouth closed.

The words her daughter most easily remembers now are the sibilant French phrases attached to ballet, so there is *plié* and *relevé* as Brianna moves slowly across the room. Maggie dresses her in tights and a black leotard, bringing her to the studio where she'd once trained as a promising ballerina—one who auditioned for *the rock school, did you hear that, my girl was picked before any of your daughters*—but now her girl limps broken, a fumbling child with wide doll eyes. A hope: that her daughter's body and mind suddenly remember the room and the music and the feel of the instructor's hands on her flesh, forming the muscles into all the old familiar shapes. They are alone here, Maggie and her daughter and the instructor, it is late at night after the studio closes, but Maggie thinks it's probably better that way. The other parents look at her with pity that makes her angry. It makes her want to smack her own child in the head so that something might break loose, like a record player needle looping in a deep scratch.

She watches from a corner chair and plays the past in her head. She's been doing a lot of that the past few weeks, sitting up late at night in bed with the old home movies, the volume on the television muted so she won't wake her husband. Even with a fat baby belly, her daughter had always been petite and pretty, her profile showing off a nose so dainty that Maggie had wondered how it could possibly smell anything, had sworn that it must be strictly ornamental. When those tiny rosebud lips would part, Brianna's voice was shrill and demanding. As an infant, Brianna had spoken long before she could walk, sentences like *mama want milk* and *mama no nap* and *mama look, mama look at baby*, and Maggie had given into those demands because how could she not? Mother meaning caregiver, mother meaning nurturer, mother meaning I put you before all others—I will give you all the best parts of myself.

On the floor, her daughter's legs kick at the air, the *battements*, muscles running down her calves marking time like a metronome.

en dehors, then *en dehans*, and again—from the front of the body to the back, the movement of the mind like soup from one memory to the next, pouring out from an unseen leak in her daughter's brain until the simplest words and phrases have disappeared. Until her memory has run dry as an empty snow globe, all the little bits of plastic clinking together and breaking.

Movies on loop, forever, *did you see that, did you see me do that, mommy,* recitals where the other little girls and her daughter showcased all of the new things that their bodies had been conditioned to know. *hey mommy, did you see me,* baby daughter in pink tights that dragged down her chubby little legs until she yanked them back up from the crotch, saying *but that's where they're falling down, mommy,* and how after the recitals they would go out for brunch, but her daughter would only eat the pancakes if they had a face made out of cut up bits of fruit; the banana sliced neat like slick coins for the gigantic smile.

Her husband hadn't wanted to pay for the dance lessons. Money was tight with two kids in the house, and Brian had been allergic to everything—they'd had to buy the special detergent and baby formula, and the little extra money they'd had leftover her husband had wanted to save for a family vacation, but she'd been adamant. *look at those feet,* she'd said, pointing out the high arches and the delicate ankles. *my daughter is a dancer.*

Now they weren't paying for lessons, but they were paying for specialists—neurologists and doctors who couldn't explain the sudden memory loss, not a brain tumor, not anything like that, but no one could tell them what was happening. It had started slow, forgetting appointments and homework, like any other teenager, but then it had avalanched into forgetting faces and people and the word for dog or cat or tree or sometimes even forgetting her own name—B R I A N N A, the name she'd learned how to write with a fat crayon when she'd been less than four years old. Maggie wondered if it was psychological, thought that maybe some traumatic event had triggered a panicked regression.

what if she'd been raped? She'd had to whisper this to her husband, in the dark, in the safety of her bedroom, because she couldn't bear to think of anyone else hearing the words. *what if someone hurt her?* But there was no way to prove that was true. It could just as easily have been the result of some lingering illness, or a genetic abnormality that finally decided to show itself, something that had incubated in her daughter's head like a burrowing parasite, growing fat off her daughter's brain.

Things she did not say out loud: *what if it was something I did, what if it was from the time she rolled off the bed when I was changing her clothes when she was three months old, what if it was from something I fed her, what if it's because I didn't make her wash her hands in that public restroom?*

Brianna bends at the waist and then stretches up to the ceiling, fingers flexing, the muscled line of her back mirrored at Maggie's face. She can see every nuance of her daughter's body. Over the years it has curved and strengthened and become a stranger's body, first through puberty, and now a stranger to everyone, including herself. Sometimes Maggie will catch her daughter staring in the mirror with a terrified look, as if she doesn't recognize her own face.

When the instructor leaves, she pats Maggie on the shoulder and it feels like one of the doctors saying *we've done all that we could*. She goes to collect her daughter, who is spinning slow circles in the center of the room.

"My baby, it's time to go home." She puts her hand on Brianna's shoulder and her daughter laughs and twirls away.

"Á terré," Brianna says. Her face is shiny with sweat and tendrils of hair curl by her temples. She smells like a puppy that's been playing outside. "Dégagé."

Then her daughter's arms are around her waist and they are smoothly moving together across the floor. To the mirror, across the middle, no clearly defined destination, just a movement from one place to another.

effacé, obscured, hidden from view

Back in the middle of the floor, they stand linked together, Maggie's arms around her daughter's neck, her daughter's arms around her waist. They sway back and forth. Maggie hums the music from the Nutcracker under her breath, and Brianna asks what the song is from.

"It's your favorite," Maggie says. "The Dance of the Sugar Plum Fairy. You love it."

"Hair, mother hair." Brianna touches either side of Maggie's face. "Gone."

As they spin in smaller, tighter circles, Maggie thinks that maybe her daughter is moving backward in time to start all over again—that memory loss is a precursor to a complete loss of self, so that maybe Maggie can just tuck her daughter back up inside the womb and cook her up all over again. This time she'll make sure to prepare everything just right, a cake batter with the perfect ingredients to insure a successful delivery.

Maggie stops humming and they stand pressed together, bodies posed like two kids at prom.

"Again," Brianna says. "Mother, again."

Blessing of the Animals

Moira wanted to make a joke about animals going two-by-two when they pulled into the church parking lot, but unsurprisingly her girlfriend beat her to it.

"*Je*-sus Christ," Jasmine muttered, easing their battered Cherokee past the line that wrapped around the church building and spilled out into the street. "When should we expect the flood?"

The parade started at the back parking lot of Grace Baptist, winding its way through the hedges that bracketed the breezeway. Moira waved to a few people she knew, but it was mostly a sea of unfamiliar faces. They clutched guinea pigs, turtles, and assorted birds. There was an elderly man holding a large wooden crate full of white rats, leaning against the building to disperse the weight against his thighs. Dogs in every hue wove between bodies, tangled up in their leashes. Everyone clumped together, mostly congregating on the small lawn between the choir room and the sanctuary. On this side of the building, the overlarge stained glass windows depicted the last supper, Jesus preparing the miracle of the yellow-and-orange loaves and the turquoise-and-green fishes.

After circling the lot twice and swearing loud enough that Moira cranked up her window, Jasmine finally found a spot at the back corner next to a bright green dumpster that divided the church from a Sonny's BBQ restaurant. Their lot was mostly empty in the late afternoon hours between lunch and dinner. The air was redolent with the smoky aroma of mesquite and the sweeter underlying odor of warm garbage.

Moira opened the visor mirror to fix her hair, which had blown out of its pins on the drive over. When she got out of the car, she also checked the back of her skirt. She'd put on a heavy pad, which seemed like overkill with a menstrual cup, but you could never tell with a bad period. It felt a little like she was wearing a diaper; there was a crinkling noise like scrunched wrapping paper coming from between her legs.

"You can't hear that, can you?" She took a few steps forward and then back again to show off the sound. To Moira's ears, it was horribly loud.

"I can't hear anything. Why did you even wear that?"

"Just in case." Moira adjusted her skirt and then her underwear, which had slipped a little to the side. "I like to be prepared."

"Cutest Girl Scout in central Florida."

Moira checked her purse one more time to make sure she hadn't forgotten any of her papers. They were all there: the pre-marriage counseling documents she'd printed off the internet, the wedding service itinerary. She ruffled them with her fingers and pushed the folder back down inside, zipping the bag closed.

"Where to?" Jasmine asked. "This is your deal." Moira frowned and Jasmine put up a hand, smiling. "I don't mind, you know that. Just lead the way."

She pointed toward the direction of the line and started forward into the mass of people, Jasmine following along behind her.

Pastor Mark's office was at the back of the church. They picked their way through the crowd, which was overrun with small children and animals. Some people held their pets in carriers and others in their arms, heaved over shoulders like burped babies. A black and white potbelly pig rooted in a patch of weeds, snuffling wetly, an oak leaf stuck to its snout. Nearby a skinny Siamese on a gold rhinestone leash flattened itself to the ground, crawling on its belly toward an open drainage grate. Some kids playing with a cocker spaniel laughed and pointed as the cat fought to get loose, working one shoulder free before getting trapped and yowling fitfully. His owner struggled to detangle the leash while simultaneously avoiding the flailing claws, hissing when one finally landed in her neck, scraping a hot pink line.

"Excuse us, excuse me. I'm sorry," Moira repeated over and over again, pushing through the swarm until she felt lightheaded. A border collie chasing a big black lab brushed against Moira's legs, nearly knocking her over. Both dogs yipped wildly, excited to be outside among all the smells. They ran a little too close to the street and a sedan swerved to avoid hitting them. The driver lay on the horn and threw up a middle finger.

"Watch out for dog shit," Jasmine said, and Moira shushed her.

It was bright out, mid-March in Florida, so the weather wasn't as bad as it could have been. Moira wore a blue cotton sundress and low-slung heels that sunk in the grass with every step, but she wished she'd put on something nicer. Maybe worn her khaki suit, the one with the plaid lining and matching pencil skirt. Even just a silk slip or some nylons.

Some of the people they squeezed past were dressed up, but most of them just had on shorts or jeans. It was warm and very humid. Moira nodded quickly at a few people. She'd been a member of the church for four years; she knew many of the families from Sunday service. Closest to the building were the Delancetts with their gray schnauzer, Bucky, who jumped athletically at an elderly couple escorting a fluffy white Persian. There was Tom Brackin holding a portable aquarium for his eight-year-old daughter, Denisa, who played on her iPhone in the shade of the building. She waved off clouds of gnats with her free hand. Moira called hello to her as they slipped inside the building, but the girl never looked up from the screen.

Inside the church was marginally cooler. Moira pulled her dress away from her armpits and winced at the heaviness in her pelvis. Her period was bad this month, nearly doubling her over before she'd gotten in the car to leave that afternoon. She'd chased a palm full of Ibuprofen with a swig of warm soda and tossed the keys to Jasmine. The painkillers had helped, but not much. She felt slightly feverish and her joints ached, as if she might have caught the flu.

Straight ahead was the threshold that led them into the sanctuary or down the hall, into the back church offices. For a moment, Moira paused. She really did need to go, but she had on the pad and the closest bathroom was at the other end of the church. After a second's pause, she decided she could wait. She turned down the long hall filled with heavy framed portraits of former church leaders, Olan Mills photography with clear glaze brush over top to look like oil paintings. A small oak table set beside an open doorway held an aggressively green fake Ficus and a copy of the church brochure. Pastor Mark smiled whitely from its cover. He'd been superimposed onto an overly pixelated photograph of the church building. WELCOME TO OUR FAMILY! it said in bold yellow font, Pastor Mark's hand outstretched as if he were inviting you inside the brochure itself.

Once through the door, the church secretary let them into Pastor Mark's office. Brenda ushered them into overstuffed chairs with the same blue fabric they'd used to upholster the pews in the sanctuary two years ago. Jasmine was wearing a sundress too, a pink one with spaghetti straps that she'd borrowed from Moira. Jasmine was not a dress person; the closest she'd owned was a pleather miniskirt from a previous Halloween costume. The pink dress was a little loose in the waist and bust, so they'd covered it up with a bulky white cardigan unearthed from the back of Moira's side of the closet. The shoulders had weird, conical pads inside that they'd clipped out with scissors. It sagged off Jasmine's shoulders like an old afghan.

Sun shone in through the window and lit both their faces in stripes. "I should have shaved my legs this morning." Jasmine scrubbed a fidgety hand through her short hair and it stuck up on the side. Moira reached over to smooth it down, but then the door opened so she put her hand back in her lap.

Pastor Mark wore dark jeans and a navy polo. Moira thought his face looked slightly pained, as if he were in the middle of a particularly stressful dental procedure. Moira was a dental hygienist.

She knew that look—it was the kind little kids made right before they bit her fingers.

"What was it you wanted to discuss, Moira?" His lips were shiny, as if he'd just put on ChapStick. "As you can see, we've got a big day ahead of us."

"Yeah, what's with all that, anyway?" Jasmine's voice was gruff. Moira cleared her own throat, wishing she could do it for Jasmine.

"I told her, it's the animal blessing, but she doesn't really get it." Moira laughed and immediately wished she hadn't. "She hasn't been to church that often; her family's *lapsed Catholic*." That last she said in a kind of whisper, leaned in toward Pastor Mark. "I'm hoping I can get her to start coming here with me."

He nodded. "Right. Well, we're doing a special blessing today—an animal blessing; something brand new for us. We're actually the first in our city to try this out." He kept on talking, not expecting a response, though Jasmine still looked confused. "People are bringing all their pets in for it; we're hoping that it'll get people motivated to come join our church family." Pastor Mark really smiled at this, and Moira saw that his teeth looked a lot less white than they did on the brochure.

Jasmine frowned. "So you're gonna baptize dogs and cats?"

"It's more of a special prayer service. I'll say a few psalms, pet a few furry heads. You know, keep it simple."

"Oh. That's kind of cool." Jasmine grabbed Moira's hand and Moira tried not to flinch. It was hard not to when she could see Pastor Mark's eyes narrow in on their fingers, as if he could sense the intimate way Jasmine stroked her inner palm with her thumb.

"We don't want to take up too much of your time." Moira pulled back her hand and grabbed for the folder she'd left beneath her padded chair. She set it in her lap, fiddling with the edge until it rolled backward, the thick paper separating at the seam. "I—*we*—wanted to speak with you about having our service at the church."

"What type of service?"

Barking started up outside the window, quickly morphing into a high, whining yelp, and the bushes rattled and brushed the window screen. A woman's face appeared in the greenery, wide with bright pink spots high on her cheekbones. *Sorry*, she mouthed through the glass. She held up a fluffy white dog with brown gunk around its eyes, and then waved the dog's paw apologetically.

"A wedding service." Moira said, still staring at the waving paw. The dog looked old and mournful. "*Our* service."

Pastor Mark folded his arms over the lip of his desk, fingers tapping his wrist. There was a dark red crease in his neck, a place that looked a little chapped, like maybe he'd brushed against it a little too hard with his razor that morning. He opened his mouth, and then closed it again.

Moira rushed ahead. "I know you guys do all kinds of services. Never this kind, but other kinds. Second marriages, third marriages. Blended families. I mean, I've even helped with a few—the Ruebens last month, I worked kitchen duty." She threw a quick, quivery smile his way. "This is my family, you know? And I want my ceremony at my home church."

In the silence that followed, Moira tried to regulate her breathing. She stared hard at the divot between his eyebrows, not at a point where she felt confident enough to look in his eyes directly. Jasmine fiddled with the latch on her purse, clicking it open and closed. Pastor Mark looked down at his desk calendar, and then back up at Moira.

"You're right; this isn't something we've done before." He cleared his throat. "But as you know, our administration is open to moving in . . . contemporary . . . directions, as long as it's handled discreetly and with dignity."

Moira suppressed a frown; the word dignity made her think of a funeral. Jasmine sat looking out the window, nonplussed. Unlike Moira, who'd dreamed of a big church wedding since she was a little girl, Jasmine had never really wanted to get married and didn't care about a service either way. When Moira had tentatively brought it up, Jasmine had just shrugged and gone along with it, humoring Moira like she always did. Jasmine was the relaxed one, the one who could compromise, unlike Moira, whose shoulders were always tense from stress.

Pastor Mark was still talking. "Obviously we can't do the regular stuff, but we can try and work around that. What date were you and Ms . . . " he trailed off, looking pointedly at Jasmine.

"Bota," Jasmine supplied. "B-O-T-A."

Pastor Mark nodded and scribbled something on the corner of his desk calendar.

"What date were you and Ms. Bota considering? We also need to make sure that there's not already a conflict, but I can just check with Brenda for that."

"So . . . we won't need to do the prerequisite counseling sessions?" Moira asked, pulling the papers from her folder. It was all stuff her friend Meghan had to do before her ceremony at the church. Several weeks' worth of counseling sessions. There was even a workbook you had to buy; Moira had already ordered two copies. "I thought those were mandatory?"

"It usually is, but this is a . . . different kind of ceremony, right? So we can just skip it. You all have a . . . person that can run the service for you?"

"Well, no," Moira said, anxiety ramping up. "I thought you did them."

She'd seen him in action, beautifully crafted lines that showed he knew the couple intimately. He was charming on stage, a smooth hand with the bible and juggling the rings. This was why she'd wanted the ceremony; so she could have the idyllic service that she'd been focused on her whole life. She'd mapped it all out in her head—the dress, the bridesmaids, the flowers. The same thing everyone else got to have.

Pastor Mark frowned. "Oh no, I've never done this kind of ceremony before. We wanna make sure you get someone who knows what they're doing. We can put you in the gymnasium, too. Much more casual for something like this, right?"

Jasmine patted her hand, picking up the conversation as Moira struggled to answer. "Okay, we can do that. We're looking at June sixteenth—it's a Saturday."

Pastor Mark turned to his computer and clicked open a program on his desktop. "Day or evening?"

Moira twisted her hands in her lap.

Brenda walked in with an overflowing cardboard box of forms. "Sorry to interrupt, Pastor Mark, but the paperwork is really piling up. It's getting wild out there."

Moira's neck was sweaty beneath the fall of her hair, which refused to stay in her pins. She could smell her hairspray; cloying, an artificial wildflower scent that overpowered everything else in the room. "I have to use the bathroom," she blurted. "I'll be right back." She didn't wait for a response, just up and walked to the door. Her throat felt tight, like someone had clenched a hand around it.

There were no windows at the rear of the church. As she crossed the darkly shaded hallway, she took deep breaths and dug through her purse for some Advil. Her cramps were suddenly ferocious, a gnawing animal in her guts that wouldn't let up. She wished she was home with the hot rice pack over her pelvis, lying down flat on her couch watching reality television.

A few people sat in the back pew of the sanctuary before the double doors leading out into the vestibule. She recognized them: it was Rita Lowell and her little girl, Stephanie, holding a small red and blue shoebox. Rita was patting the girl's shoulders and smoothing down her long brown hair as Stephanie bent forward over her lap, arms crossed around her knees.

Moira couldn't respond to the woman's smile. She walked straight past and pushed through the door into the vestibule, which was brightly lit and warm from big windows at either side. The women's restroom was open; it looked like someone had been in to clean it recently. The wooden stop was pressed down flush between the door frame and the pale blue carpet. She kicked it out with the toe of her shoe. The stop skid across the tile and careened into the wall with a sharp bang. The door slid slowly closed behind her.

There's a fifty percent chance I'll throw up, Moira thought. The room smelled like lemon disinfectant, but there was also the strong underlying odor of waste, as if someone had been in just before her with an upset stomach.

No matter that she'd had a regular menstrual cycle since she was twelve; it was still strange when she had her period. Her body was suddenly alien, a thing that hurt and pulsed and stretched without reason. Her stomach bloated until her pants felt like a too-tight elastic band, water weight exacerbated by incredible salt cravings. She could eat an entire bag of chips in a single sitting and then get up and open another. This type of eating also worsened her skin, adding a patchwork of underground cystic acne to her face that made it hurt to smile or even press her face to her pillow.

Inside the bathroom, the stalls were the color of cooked salmon. The wall tiles the same shade, but lighter and opalescent, as if they'd splurged on something a little more upscale. All the grout on the floor was dark and stained. She pulled up her dress and squatted over the toilet, pulling the sweaty pad free of the crotch of her underpants and stuffing it into the small metal garbage bin attached to the wall. For the past few months she'd been using the menstrual cup, but it wasn't really working out. They were what Jasmine used, and she'd told Moira they were a godsend. In fact, Jasmine had talked it up so much that she'd felt like she was in the middle of a menstrual cup commercial—at any minute she'd expected to talk about brownies and chocolate or for someone to pour blue liquid over a sanitary pad.

"My period is *so* easy now." Jasmine had placed her hand over her womb, as if the small plastic cup were a baby percolating inside her pelvis. "I can barely feel anything; I only have to change like twice a day. It's insane!"

Her menstrual cup had come with instructions written in pastel pink and purple, and she'd read them cover to cover, religiously, attempting to memorize what she'd need to do to insert and remove. "But what if I'm out somewhere," she'd asked. "I can't just do that in a public bathroom."

"Sure you can. You just dump it out, and put it back in."

"What about the blood? Won't it get everywhere?" Moira envisioned a scene from the end of *The Shining*; the one where the elevator opened up and spilled buckets of blood all over the hotel carpet.

"No. Don't be crazy."

"But it's weird, right? Putting it up there yourself? Digging it back out?"

"We put our hands on each other like that," Jasmine replied. "We put our hands *in* each other, right?"

Moira had wanted to believe her. She'd agreed to give the cup a solid three months, but her cramps, always bad, were worse than ever. It was as if they could feel the cup, a plastic, alien invader, and her uterus pushed back angrily. The cramps were nearly debilitating, always if she were stressed out and anxious. Especially this weekend, sitting in her Pastor's office, surrounded by a menagerie of zoo animals and her girlfriend in an outfit that looked like a little girl playing dress up.

This would be here first public restroom changing. Moira followed the directions. She squatted over the church toilet and pressed down with her pelvic muscles, like she was going to the bathroom, and reached into herself to twist it loose. As the cup pulled free of her body with its strange, uncomfortable suction, her fingers involuntarily squeezed. Blood ran everywhere, down the sides of her hand, and onto her knee and calf, leaking down into her shoe.

"Fuck, shit! Fuck!" Her whispers banged off the bathroom tile, the bathroom of her church, and she bit her lip and spread her thighs as wide as she could still trapped by the web of her underwear, dumping the remainder in the toilet and dousing her inner thighs with crimson as well.

Blood had dripped on the skirt of her pale blue dress, leaving polka dots that spread along the fabric. Moira hurriedly stuck the cup on top of the dispenser and grabbed a fistful of toilet paper, swabbing her legs, and wrapping some of it around the crotch of her underwear. When she squeezed, red bloomed through immediately.

She knew there was a tampon in the bottom of her purse, somewhere down where the checkbook and her extra pack of mint gum lived. Standing up, she grabbed it off the hook at the back of the door and set it between her feet next to a clot of blood the size of a nickel. When she found the tampon, the package was unwrapped on one end. Lint had infiltrated the cardboard applicator. For half a second, she wondered what the complications could be from sticking a half opened tampon into herself—*toxic shock syndrome, some kind of flesh-eating bacteria*—then quickly inserted it.

Toilet paper dragged over her arm as she unlooped more and more, squeezing at the hem of her dress, then wiping at herself and her underwear, stuffing a bit into her shoe to try and get the drip that had leaked down into her pump. She wrapped the stained plastic cup in a huge wad of it until it looked like she'd gift-wrapped a present. This she stuffed down into her purse, before wiping her hands the best that she could, and swiping at the floor with some toilet paper remnants that she dumped in the toilet.

Exiting the stall, Moira dropped her purse on the shelf over the sink and looked at her face in the spotty mirror. Her skin was pale, making her lipstick look just a tad too pink. Dark eye makeup had smudged up under the corners of her eyes. Moira ripped paper towels from the rack and clumped them in a ball beside her bag before lifting her skirt and putting it directly under the tap. There was a hand dryer in the corner—if she could rinse out enough of the blood with soap and cold water, then she could hold the fabric under the vent to dry it. Then she might actually make it back out to the meeting before anyone realized something was wrong.

There were voices outside the door right before it banged open, slamming hard against the wall. Moira dropped her dress and crossed her hands over her crotch, worried that she'd been caught exposing herself. Stephanie and her mother, Rita, walked in carrying the shoebox. Stephanie was really crying now, the kind where no sound came out. They walked over to the sink beside Moira. She turned her body so that her front was pushed up against the lip of the porcelain, hoping they would leave soon so that she could finish cleaning herself up. She smoothed some of her hair back from her forehead and avoided eye contact in the mirror.

"You just need to calm down, honey. Let's wash your face. Get you feeling better."

"No! I want Wallace."

There wasn't any soap left in the dispenser. Moira pushed the plastic lever again and again with her palm, hoping for even a little wisp of foam, but it was just air. Stephanie was producing little hiccupping coughs that flecked spit down her chin,

"I think they might be out of soap again," Rita said, jerking her thumb at the cabinet in the corner. "Kids keep coming in and messing around with them. If you wait a second, I'll try and find the refill bottle."

Stephanie wiped an arm against her runny nose.

"No, sweetheart, not your cardigan. Let's get you a tissue." When Rita tried to take the shoebox, Stephanie yelled and jerked it. There was no lid and the contents spilled out: a blue and white bandana and a little ball of sandy colored fuzz dumped at Moira's feet.

Moira reached down and grabbed the bundle, picking up what looked like a former hamster. He was in a solid state, rigor firmly curling his limbs into a permanent fetal position. She held him out to Stephanie in her cupped palm.

"Let me just take him from you," Rita said, her voice a little pinched, and that's when Moira noticed all the blood that still clung to her hands and fingernails, some of it staining up the coat of the hamster. Rita picked up the animal awkwardly with two fingers; the hamster body stiff as a small stuffed toy.

Wallace was replaced in the box and Rita walked up to the sink to rinse her own hands, throwing on the faucet and flecking off the excess water until it dotted the mirror. "Stephie, honey, can you go ahead back out there and maybe sit with Denisa?"

As Stephanie walked out with the box clutched to her chest, Jasmine came into the bathroom. "What's taking so long, are you okay?"

"Here, use this." Rita pulled a detergent pen from her purse and uncapped it. She shook it a few times, the ball bearing inside making a loud clacking noise. "I have this problem all the time, when my pads leak. This thing is like a lifesaver, I carry it everywhere."

Jasmine took off the white sweater and handed it to Moira. "Put this around your waist."

Moira let Rita dab at the stain on the hem of her dress while she scrubbed at her hands with plain water. The sweater was heavy against her stomach and dragged her dress off one shoulder; her beige bra strap showed light against her freckled skin. She thought it looked a little stained and hoped that Rita hadn't noticed.

"Just use the bar since the other's out." Rita pointed with the pen and then got back to doodling at Moira's hem.

There was a hard bar of soap, sitting up on the rack— dehydrated and cracked enough to resemble split skin. Moira had to froth it under the tap awhile before it would lather. She dug in her fingernails until the soap caked there whitely like caulk.

"There, that's much better." Rita dropped the dress and Moira felt the cold wetness on her thigh with revulsion, like the shock of pulling back on a damp bathing suit.

"Thank you," she said, but the other woman had already turned away to wash her hands with the bar.

Jasmine and Moira walked through the bathroom door, one after the other, while Rita stayed behind to refill the empty dispensers. In the vestibule, a pile of people lined up, walking through the double door of either side of the sanctuary. There was a pee stain on the ground that the crowd parted around. One of the deacons was already kneeling beside it, scrubbing with a small plastic brush. The yellow bristles were bleached out on the tips.

Overhead the speakers let in the crackling voice of Pastor Mark, who was leading the assembled congregation from behind the pulpit. There was a dog in his arms, what looked like a fat little golden retriever puppy. "The beatitudes were just made for these beautiful creatures," he said, holding up the dog's paw and waving it out at the crowd. Everyone collectively oohed in approval. There were several other very sweet looking puppies held up at the front of the sanctuary.

"Blessed are the pure in heart, amen." Pastor Mark handed off the puppy to Brenda, who was waiting on the step below, and then grabbed for a wicker basket of kittens. Moira could hear them mewing, tiny little soft sounds like they were still being weaned.

"Are we going to finish our meeting?" she asked. Jasmine shook her head and pulled her through the crowd clumped at the entrance and on the stairs that led out front.

Outside the air was warm and fragrant with the smell of damp grass. Moira took a breath and held it, glad to be away from the people and the animal smells, dander and fur and pent up perfume and recycled oxygen.

"He gave us some paperwork, we just need to fill it out send it back. Brenda can take care of the rest."

"This isn't what I wanted. It's not right."

They stopped and stood outside on the baking pavement. Jasmine squeezed her fingers. "I know it's not. But it's something. Something's better than nothing."

Moira wondered if that was true.

Little scraps of paper and garbage drifted near the gym and the border between the building and street. Moira watched a candy wrapper float up and land twice. The air felt thick in her lungs. When her stomach growled, loudly, she was shocked to realize she was hungry. She'd barely eaten lunch, too nervous about the meeting to keep down the chicken salad she'd thrown together. She didn't want to talk about it anymore. She wanted to forget it ever happened.

"Could you grab us some pork sandwiches and fries?" Moira asked. "I'll wait here. I still feel disgusting."

She climbed into the car and zoned out while Jasmine put their stuff in the backseat and then crossed over into the BBQ restaurant's parking lot, out of sight behind the big green dumpster. Moira's cramps felt a little better now. She rolled down her window, pushing her skirt between her legs as the wind ruffled through. In the side mirror, the papers that Jasmine had set down in the backseat fluttered, scattering along the floorboard.

Moira ate the first of her pork sandwiches as Jasmine piloted the car home. In between bites, she fed Jasmine some of the crinkle fries and turned on the radio. Her coke was cold with crushed ice and tasted just right. There were napkins in the bag. She wiped off her greasy face and chin, and then tossed them into the backseat along with the paper food bag. She turned up the radio when Aretha came on and sang along, loudly, until they got home. Then she picked up the garbage from the backseat and the paperwork from the floor and threw it all into the garbage bin outside their garage.

Aberrations in Flight

The summer that Elizabeth and I moved into the new house, birds dive-bombed our back windows from mid-afternoon to early evening. The thump of their bodies against the glass set up a steady rhythm to the rest of the constant noise: the screech of cicada, the yowl of the neighbor's cats, and the koi pond stuffed with fat bullfrogs that regularly bellowed their sexual frustrations. The birds were our main attraction, though—screaming kamikaze pilots headed toward death on our double-glazed panes. In between their aerial feats, they perched at our cracked ceramic birdbath, covens of jays and crows, wrens, swifts and the occasional cardinal. They pecked incessantly at the crumbling ceramic until the yard was full of crunchy white dandruff. They splattered our cars with shit, nested in the eaves of our house, and loudly fought each other over insects. After only a month, their squawking was the noise I most associated with homeownership.

According to our friends, summer was the perfect time to move. We sat in their dining rooms and ate up their advice along with burgers that had been grilled out on their patios. We were told the market was down, that there would never be a better time to buy. How could we possibly expect to move once fall hit and everything great was snatched up?

There was no arguing that the timing was ideal. We both held established careers with summers off: Elizabeth was a high school art teacher and I was on faculty at the local college. We were two years into our relationship and homeownership felt like a natural progression. Neither of us had ever owned property before, but the realtor had been reassuring.

On the scuffed-beyond-repair parquet: "Quaint."

The closet-sized third bedroom: "Cozy."

A hole in the roof over the back porch where a rat had chewed through the ductwork: "We can work that into the contract."

I'd never lived somewhere with so many bathrooms. Growing up, there'd been one toilet shared between our family. Sitting on the throne, your knees hit the lip of the fiberglass bathtub. We'd lived on top of each other in a single-story ranch, its floors nearly concave thanks to the damp and the Florida aquifer. Since moving out, I'd lived in apartments exclusively. They were spare places with fluorescent lighting and very thin walls, cluttered with disposable furniture made from MDF. These apartments were convenient, but the constant interaction with neighbors had annoyed me. Food smells from their units would filter through the cracks in our door, scenting our apartment with curry or cinnamon, cheeseburgers or pizza. Twice our air conditioning had broken and it had taken over a week to fix, while we sweltered in t-shirts and underwear and kept the blinds down over our open windows. Now there were wide hedges and a big yard, a picket fence that ran the perimeter of the property. Elizabeth said I coveted the privacy more than the extra bathrooms. She was right. Never again would I have to make awkward small talk on a stairwell when I went to pick up the mail. It popped through a slot in my front door and waited for me on the entryway rug.

The new house was located midway between our jobs, with a long, curving drive and a wide brick exterior. Most of the houses charm came with caveats bridged with the word "but." Our kitchen had new cabinets, but the appliances were all from the late sixties—coppers and browns, oranges and sunburst reds, warm colors for an oven that wouldn't heat above 250 degrees. The bedrooms all had tray ceilings, but their floors came with two layers of carpet: shag and dog hair. The scent of urine was especially strong in the back bedroom where the windows had magnified the sun, cooking up squares of carpeting. A beautiful old fireplace sat in our sunken living room, but when the home inspector came out and prodded around inside the chimney, an entire family of bats skittered out. We'd had to call an exterminator before we could go back inside.

We negotiated the owners down ten thousand dollars due to the repairs, but we didn't mind a fixer upper. It was the original charm of the house we sought as we lovingly scraped and prodded at the "vintage" portions. Some new, some old. We let the bathrooms keep their salmon pink tile, but I drew the line at faucets that drooled down the backs of the pipes. In all three bathrooms, much of the original millwork had already gone spongey, white wood sagging beneath our assorted toiletries. Even the slight odor of mildew and the dark splotches of mold couldn't deter our enthusiasm. We were *homeowners*.

That first week I played house in cargo shorts, hung a hammer from the loop in my pants and threw nails in my pockets. I hung picture frames and mirrors, installed pre-fabricated shelves in our musty pantry. Elizabeth made us picnic dinners of cold cuts and pretzel sticks, and we drank lukewarm cans of beers in the middle of our empty dining room floor as we watched the sun sink through the trees in our front yard. It was a vacation from real life, putting down area rugs and picking out paint samples, buying outlet plates and new lamps for the guest bedrooms.

When a sudden thunderstorm blew a huge collection of branches onto our roof, I had to climb up afterward and drag them off by myself, crouched nervously along the lip, worried I'd fall off and break my neck. I found places where the roofing shingles were loose and the material underneath crumbled like wet sawdust. Constant rain caused a puddle near a large crack in the front door, and I had to buy weather stripping. The parquet in the kitchen pulled up, and I bought adhesive to flatten it back out, but everything was just too damp and it slid loose underfoot every few days. An infestation of roaches boiled up from the cupboards; one small egg housed nearly fifty babies and they'd spread out into all the cracks and crevices of the woodwork. A new problem every day, and I couldn't fix any of them.

My father had effortlessly mended doorframes, shaving down the wood when it swelled fat from humidity. He knew how to use WD-40 on a bike chain, on a jammed lock, on a rusty hinge. He owned a large spade-like flyswatter nicknamed Vince that could kill a palmetto bug in mid-flight. Elizabeth didn't know how to fix the sagging caulk line in the guest bathroom and neither did I, though I went out and bought a tube of the stuff and jammed the crack full until it bled white.

"That doesn't look right."

"Yeah, no shit."

I'd been working on the crack for forty minutes and it looked terrible, icing smeared on a cake of pink tile. Half a foot of disjointed inlay and I couldn't even manage to patch it; what hope was there that anything else could get fixed? I pointed the caulking gun at her, turning it into a hostage situation. I couldn't be in charge of fixing everything.

"Then you fix it, you're the artist."

"That's not my job!"

It wasn't mine, either. Whose job was it? Who was in charge of handling stuff like a car breaking down? Which one of us was expected to kill a giant spider in the middle of night? After the first month, it began to sink in—this was not a vacation home, it was ours. Forever. We had wooed it, loved it, and married it. Leaky pipes and a squeaky back door, in sickness and in health. I stopped unpacking, tired of looking at the boxes lumped up against the walls. Mounds, the two of us carving crooked pathways out of them from the dining room to the kitchen, from the kitchen to the living room, from the living room to the bedroom.

"Let's unpack one a day. Just one box." For Elizabeth, working piecemeal was a way to make any work digestible. Break it up into small bites and you could somehow choke it down.

"Yeah, I can do that." She knew that I would not.

The summer sucked my energy. I went to my office twice a week, then once a week, trickling down to once the entire month of

July. Outside was hot and I wanted to use that as an excuse for why I hadn't gone over to the college to work on my research, but the truth was that the house rang at my brain like the bell of an ice cream truck. Elizabeth took on a summer camp course, teaching art to fourth and fifth graders who brought home structures made of toothpicks and marshmallows to their proud parents. I wondered about her days, but I never brought her a lunch like I might've done the year before, and I didn't even ask about the kids or her coworkers.

Every night she got home we sat in different rooms and fell asleep on couches and chairs, exhausted from the heat and the idea of work. I mocked up work agendas on spreadsheets and never kept any of my deadlines. I took naps every afternoon that lasted for hours, bundled up in old quilts on the couch while the television sang me to sleep.

Despite the humidity, I escaped outdoors more and more often. There was no hurry to make the yard presentable; much of it was taken care of by the constant rain of early summer, a time when grass grew whether you liked it or not. Everything came up neon green and the smell was heavy like the rubbery dirt scent of a garden hose. On the mornings I'd pull the garbage cans and recycling bins back up to the house, their wheels left deep drag marks that followed me all the way around to the side yard. The bahiagrass drove me especially crazy, its V shape waving at me like fingers when I'd pull my car up the driveway. They replicated and spread, no matter how many I yanked, five more sprouting up in place of the one I'd already cut down.

Elizabeth and I bought a mower at a garage sale, but we didn't know how to use it. It was a source of contention, harder to work than any logic puzzle. It took hours to figure out where the gas went, how to turn on the ignition, locate the pull—then gauge how hard to yank it without breaking the cord or losing it in the oil. Two women with multiple degrees crouched over its flat plastic body, too embarrassed to admit we had no clue what we were doing. When it finally belched black exhaust and self-propelled its first few feet across our yard, it was as if my own child had just taken its first steps.

"Why don't you know how to work this?" Elizabeth asked, sweaty hair clinging to her neck. There was dirt sprinkled in her cleavage. "Didn't you live on a farm?"

"A farm? Like did I work a tractor?" I laughed. "Do you think I milked a cow?"

"I don't know, I thought you did."

Elizabeth knew nothing of my family, had hardly any knowledge of my life prior to college. My childhood had mostly consisted of domestic activities. I'd taken sewing classes in a local woman's house and knew how to darn socks. I learned to bake when I was still shorter than the kitchen counter, knew how to make a piecrust with rendered lard without burning the edges. I knew how much sugar you put in the tea before it turned cloudy and thick, but I couldn't operate a weed whacker.

My brother had known how to mow a lawn since he was ten years old, sweating alongside my father while my mother mixed up watery grape Kool-Aid in the jug, plopping in square cubes of ice from the refillable plastic trays. I offered to take it out to them just so I could escape house chores. I watched my brother collect bunched clippings in a big plastic garbage bag, my father amputating the dying limbs of the crepe myrtle, slicing delicately at the twined brush so that it would grow back lush and more resilient the next spring. Drowsy in the heat, I gathered the small air potatoes from the edge of the yard in the pockets of my shorts. I liked to feed them to my family of dolls, though my mother would smack me if she caught me touching them. She claimed they were toxic.

My jobs were sweeping and dusting, drying the dishes after meals. Cleaning up the bathrooms, though the boys were the ones who always peed down the sides of the bowl. The streams left sticky yellow stripes on the porcelain that had to be removed with scouring cleanser and a damp rag. As an adult, the smell of it in public restrooms always made me mad and homesick.

I told chunks of those stories to Elizabeth, but I didn't talk much about my family. Estrangement meant parceling off my personal history and packing it up, storing it in the attic of my brain. I'd sometimes pull the memories out and flip through the best ones, the ones that conjured memories that didn't hurt too much. Then I'd put them away again and pray for mildew, a leak in the box so I wouldn't have to remember anymore.

Elizabeth told stories about her childhood that involved holiday parties, pageants and plays, but she was an only child and her parents still called her every Sunday to check in. We visited them at Christmas and they sent me birthday cards with glitter inside of them that fell on the rug. They hugged me when they'd pick us up from the airport and her mother kissed me on the cheek. No matter how nice they were, I couldn't get my arms to wrap around them the right way. I wondered sometimes if people were just no good at hugging after a certain age, that maybe they turned feral like cats. You had to be held a lot as babies to ever know how to touch right.

The summer slipped away as I replaced my work projects with trips to the Home Depot, picking up more bathroom caulk, fluorescent lightbulbs, battery packs, blue painter's tape, linoleum for the mudroom. One trip I bought bags of mulch and seven pots of African violets because I thought the colors were pretty: juicy greens, purples, black. I spent an entire afternoon rooting around in the brick basins at the front of the house using tools that we'd bought in anticipation of the move—shiny aluminum with bright red plastic handles, cheap stuff that raised blisters on my hands. As I dug into the silt I uprooted a dusky brown beetle. It crawled across my hand, and when I saw it I shrieked and flung off one of my gardening gloves.

Unlike the basin's chalky dirt, the violet's pots held thick black soil that colored the tip of my finger when I pressed down inside the cup. I turned on the hose and water drowned the gray dirt in the basin, filling for ten minutes. The dampness just made the dirt slushier. I took the violets from their pots and plugged them in the mud. They sat spread apart in the planter, looking like kids wearing clothes three sizes too big for them. The flowers had wilted considerably, and I felt limp and sluggish, hardly able to move my arms enough to pat down the clumpy soil over the roots.

Elizabeth showed up from a lunch out with a co-worker, smelling like food and wearing a cotton sundress. If I touched her bare calf I knew it would feel like refrigerated flesh from the blast of the car's air conditioner. My face was hot and I wanted to rub it against her.

"How was lunch?"

"We went to Anthony's. I brought you back a slice."

My favorite restaurant. I shouldn't have cared, I wasn't even hungry. The heat made me itchy and I disliked her companion, a woman who'd once said that ladies who wore too much makeup were obviously overcompensating. I stared at my wife's shoes as I kneeled in the dirt, absurdly high heels for an afternoon lunch at a pizza parlor. Her skin looked sweet and clean. I was sprinkled with dirt. There was a sour smell coming from my armpits.

"Those are violets?"

"I thought they were cute."

They didn't look that way anymore. They were bent over sideways, crushed from the heat.

"Violets need shade, I think."

Her toes scrunched down into the pointy tips of her shoes, angry red slices of skin peeking through the gaps. Her feet were probably roasting in the heat. I hoped she was sweating and ruining the leather.

"Can you get me my sunglasses from the front seat of my car, I'm getting a migraine."

She was half-blocking the light. I wished she'd step either one way or the other. She stared down at me and squinted, wide brackets around her eyes. We were the same age but people always thought she looked younger. She still got carded at bars; they'd started using ma'am on me by the time I turned twenty-four.

"You didn't ask me what I'd like out front."

"What, you're a master gardener now?"

"No, I'd just like some say in what happens to our house."

The hair on her legs was coming in at the ankles and darkened her pores. I focused on the black dots and tried to take deep breaths so my head would stop hurting—a pulsating pain that swelled and ebbed every three seconds.

"You decide lots of things," I said.

"Like what?"

"That ugly runner in the front hallway, I let you choose that."

"Grow up, Amber."

The way that the afternoon sun hit her face made the left side disappear. Her cheek hollowed out until the curve of her jaw glowed white like a cattle skull. Her arm was braced against the house and her shadow fell down cool over me. She looked beautiful and terrible, her silhouette willowy against the bricks.

Her shape in the sun reminded me of the time my mother picked fruit from our stunted pear tree in the front yard. When she'd lifted up her arms to yank it, her shirt rode up high on her waist. A passing car laid on the horn and the man inside yelled something out the window. In that moment, she became two different women to me: someone worthy of catcalls, and my mother, a woman who wore sloppy cut off shorts and flip-flops, someone whose fingernails dug furrows into my arm when she was angry. Women were like that to me: intriguing and exhausting, multiple stories built into a single house that couldn't support the weight.

"I'm going inside," she said. "It's too damn hot."

I turned to the planter and dug my fingers back in the dirt, jabbing holes that filled with water when I removed them. Elizabeth's shadow moved away and the heat returned to my scalp, cooking my skin.

There were weeds crawling up the side of the house and into the cracks in the brick partition that I hadn't noticed before. Was there a fault in the foundation; had we bought a house that was going to break clear down the middle?

I got up and walked to the backyard where there were some spots of shade. No matter what I tried, I couldn't get the backyard seeded. There were overhanging oaks and uneven turf that led to puddles of water, drowning everything but the weeds. A thick scent of decaying plant matter and wet dirt hung over it, but there was something else too, something denser and sweet, a smell like raw meat left in a garbage can.

Sniffing the air, I stumbled around in the silty yard until I found it: a pile of dead birds. Their necks were cocked at impossible angles. A few had their beaks pressed into the earth, some stared blankly at the sky. One curled into a comma, resting off to the side like a balled fetus. They were brown and tan, mostly, with black speckles on the breast— as if a vee of them had just migrated right into the side of the house. I dug a hole at the side of the brush, but the dirt was dense and the cheap plastic handle of the spade finally cracked and broke off. I put the birds in and dumped the remaining dirt over them with my hands, forced myself not to say a prayer under my breath.

That night the sky broke open after two weeks of no rain and I thought of the violets outside, sopping wet, and hoped they'd grow into something thick and lush, just to prove Elizabeth wrong. The sound of the heavy rain made me tired, but the formaldehyde smell of the new door we'd installed on the master bathroom was overwhelming and made me sick to my stomach. I got up to eat a bowl of cereal and stood at the back picture window, watching the rain puddle over the birds' shallow grave. I fell asleep on the couch watching infomercials and had dreams about rotisserie grills and super absorbent towels.

The next weekend Elizabeth attended an art seminar out of town. I dropped her at the airport in the steely-gray dawn and handed her the sweater from my car for when she inevitably got cold on the plane. The humidity was high that morning and the windshield was beading sweat. When I lifted her suitcase from the trunk, my jeans rubbed against the side of the car and I felt the damp all the way through to my skin. I wrapped her in the cardigan and pushed my hands up under the sleeves so I could rub at my favorite place, the smooth underside of her forearms—tender blue-white and soft like bread dough. She kissed me and I tasted the coffee on her breath, smelled the leftovers of last night's sleep.

"Did you pack your phone charger?"

"Yes."

She had sleep crusted in the corner of her eye behind her glasses and there were remnants of a pillow crease etched into her temple and cheek. When I reached up behind the glass to rub away the crust, she swatted at my hand.

"Jesus, do you want to blind me?"

"Sorry."

I didn't offer to help her with her suitcase, just sat in my car and watched her pull it awkwardly behind her until she was swallowed by the automatic doors. I drove home with the windows down, hair fuzzing from the humidity. I thought that maybe it was good she'd be away for three days so I could start to like her again.

Birds flew into the windows in the late afternoon, tapping thumps at six o'clock in the evening when the sun dipped down below the eaves of the house. That weekend I swamped out the koi pond, fished out old beer bottles and wreaths of clumped Spanish moss that dripped water on my shoes like wet hair. Elizabeth had asked me not to start on any projects while she was out of town, but I'd picked up a flier from the home improvement store on one of my past trips and I wanted to try something. Let the Sunshine IN!: a how-to for simulating summer in your home through paint technique. Elizabeth's studio was bone white and I thought it could be a nice surprise if I finished it before she got back from the conference. She did some sculpture, but mostly mural work. I couldn't tell a Rembrandt from a Hirst, but I loved to hear her talk about what she liked and what she hated. Discussing art always made her swear like crazy—those fucking cyberartists with their computer generated images, goddamn photoshopping assholes.

At the home improvement store I spent a long time at the paint station, choosing swatches with names that made me hungry: Monticello Peach, Buttered Yam, Creamsicle. There were a smorgasbord of colors that would have made a delicious meal, but I couldn't decide what would look best slapped up on a wall. How often do you stare at the sun? What kind of colors meant it was setting, which colors meant a sunrise? How many layers? I wound up buying a little of everything—sampling indiscriminately from the buffet of colors, overindulging until my car was bloated with cans and brushes and trays and tarps.

I stopped at a drive-thru on the way home and picked up breakfast. I chose an assembled sandwich made from breakfast pieces: pancakes at the top and bottom, bacon in the middle, and a spongey egg shaped into a round patty. The black coffee scalded my tongue to a fuzzy piece of felt. I lugged all the cans into the back room, worrying at the roof of my mouth. Elizabeth's studio had stacked canvasses brokering the perimeter. Its wide wall of picture windows let in all the light from the yard, sun sucking through the top panes as I flipped out the white plastic tarps onto the floor, mixing up gallons of paint in a variety of ribbed trays. I edged the trim and washed the whole wall in Clementine and Butter and Sunny-Side-Up.

As the morning wore on, birds circled the yard near the overhanging oaks, chasing each other through the branches. I cleaned up the paint mess using the hose, washing off the rollers as the water sloughed like pale milk on my hands. While I sprayed down the bricks at the back door, I heard three separate thuds. The new birds were piled on top of each other, and there were other bird parts sticking out from a mound where the neighbor's cat must have dug up their corpses: wiry legs, a small feathered head, wings spread open and blanketing the rest of the remains. I kicked the topmost bird over with my foot. There were mostly more of the small brown birds, but there were also the bright blue feathers of a scrub jay. Its eyes were wide and wet, shiny black reflecting the clouded sky overhead. I dug a larger hole with a shovel and buried them all again as a clump, watched the cloud of bottle flies circle the broken earth.

The rest of the weekend I tried not to think about my research, or what Elizabeth would think of the paint I'd smeared all over her studio walls. My mother would never have painted something in our house without asking my father's opinion first. *Marriage for women meant small but happy sacrifices*, she once said. She'd liked red and he'd liked blue, and subsequently our house had been the color of a robin's egg. When she died, I brought a big bouquet of red zinnias for the top of her casket, just to make him angry. Spite flowers at my mother's funeral.

As the weekend slipped by I watched endless hours of television and let my mind wander with the flip of the remote. I waited for Elizabeth to get home and wondered what she would make me for dinner, thought about how we were out of orange juice and that I needed to pick up more toilet paper. It rained steadily every afternoon and a leak suddenly appeared in the front hall near the entryway. I stuffed a bucket beneath it and hoped that there weren't other leaks in the house that I was missing, not sure how much a new roof was going to cost us, but betting it wouldn't be cheap.

When I picked up Elizabeth from the airport I hugged her until the equilibrium came back to my body. She'd brought home artwork and I banged my shin pulling it into the trunk of the car. Back at the house I roamed our kitchen while she unpacked her clothes and used the bathroom. I opened and closed the refrigerator, washed a dirty spoon leftover in the sink and threw away a half-finished container of yogurt. When she came back out from washing up, her face was soft and pink and she smelled like the bar of fancy milled soap I'd bought specifically for guests. She picked up the artwork from where I'd set it in the hall and I watched her walk into the studio. I suddenly wished I'd picked out blue paint instead of all those syrupy sunshine colors. Elizabeth hated breakfast food.

There was no outward sign of aggression when she came back out again. I looked into her eyes and saw she was tired from her trip and from dealing with me, and though I should've understood, it just made me angry. I wanted to her to like it.

"Why don't you take a bath?" I asked.

She smiled and went to change out of her travel clothes. The faucet turned on in our bathroom and I left the house without telling her where I was going. I drove to campus to sit alone in my office, trying to get some work done.

Instead I sat for two hours and watched crows fly past an adjacent building. The computer yielded an overwhelming amount of information on birds. There were thousands of different varieties of Florida birds. I read about their migratory patterns, what they ate and how they slept, how many eggs birthed to a clutch. My family had owned dogs, scores of them. They sat in the dirt and roamed the property without collars, never allowed inside our house. Their puppies were covered in fleas. My brother and I snuck one into the house and named it Peaches because of its orangey fur. It lived in my bedroom for a week before eating half a pack of my father's cigarettes. The dog puked on several rugs and an antique chair I wasn't even allowed to sit on. My father threw it off the back porch, and when it landed in the yard it had made a noise that sounded like an old person falling, a helpless, sad sound that soured my stomach.

I stopped at a random pet store on the drive home and looked at their selection. There were parakeets and snuggled-up lovebirds, macaws, parrots with too-bright feathers that screamed whenever I accidentally brushed against their cages. The doves were solemn and sick looking, blue feathers wilted, waxy approximations of Icarus. There was an overabundance of finches: small and delicate with decisive, darting movements. I decided to buy the one that sat alone in the back of the most crowded cage. It kept pecking the other birds.

"It's an Orange Cheek."

I put my fingers through the bars of the cage and the bird flit from one side to the other with the spastic movement of a puppy. The bold spots of color on its face made it look like it was blushing.

"Creative name. Wonder how they came up with it?"

"It's for the orange cheeks."

"Right." I picked up a water bottle that matched the one in its cage. "What else do I need?"

The bird rode home in the back seat alongside bags of millet and grass seeds, sheets of floor liners and a four-way block play activity center. The clerk claimed it kept birds from grooming themselves bald. It was quiet in the car and I kept checking the rearview to make sure that the bird wasn't dead. It sat huddled at the bottom of the small white cage looking small and unhappy. I wondered if birds could get carsick.

"Did you have a girlfriend back at the pet store?"

The bird moved to a shady corner of the cage where I couldn't see him. I turned on the radio to drown out the silence.

He began to warble when I brought the cage inside. The noises were like vocal exercises. His notes trilled up and down, over and over. The sound was overwhelming in a house where most of the noise originated from the settling of old wood and the low hum of the television set. I brought him into Elizabeth's studio and was surprised to see her painting brown circles over the wall that I'd worked on all weekend. The oranges and yellows look especially crass with the darker tone muddled over them. I set the cage on an empty side table facing the back window and tried to make sense of the colors.

"Why?"

"It's my work space." Her back was to me and the line of her back was rigid. "I don't come to your job and move around the books in your office, do I?"

I stared at a handprint of paint on the back of her dress, near her ass. The fingers looked like they were cupping her through the fabric.

"I doubt you could even find it."

"Yeah, okay." She turned around and the light from the window slashed across her face horizontally from where the panes met. The dark line cut over her lip, made her look like she had a handlebar mustache.

"This is hideous," I said. I'd spent hours painting the trim alone. "Seriously. The worst."

"Stop it." Elizabeth's voice was high and sloppy. The pudding quivers of her vocal chords drove me crazy; the gyrating swoop of high to low did something to my brain, shut off my emotions. "I know you don't talk like this to your co-workers."

The brown paint dripped slowly down and she scooped it up with the bristles of her brush, painting a downward crescent.

"Just get out."

"Fine." I hoped the mural gave her an artists' block. "Do whatever you want."

The bird stayed behind in the studio, but an hour later when I went out to water the lawn the cage sat on the floor in the living room. The bird looked lost and unkempt, and I didn't have the heart to name him. He wasn't a Theodore or a Pretty Boy or a Tweety. He was just a regular bird, like all the others. Nothing special.

I began to think about birds all day, but especially in the dreamy space between sleep and awake. Their fluttering and thumping followed me all over the house. I heard them while showering in the small cave of our master bath, or when I brewed coffee. Reading out on the porch, I listened to differentiate their calls as I holed up in the small square of shade beside our solitary fruit tree—a gnarled orange that grew beautiful fruit, all bitter from a past freeze.

I slid my feet under the chair as ants began their slow descent into the cavities of downed fruit. Brown lizards perched in the bushes, necks bouncing jaggedly as the sunset crests of their necks flexed. Birds flew in irregular patterns overhead, small gray shadows bouncing along the ground. One bird swooped upward from the window glass at the very last second—a pilot with a death wish.

Signs popped up around our neighborhood advertising an estate sale for an elderly couple who'd moved to a retirement village. I wandered around in the afternoon heat, picking through the leftovers that wouldn't fit their new condo lifestyle. Nothing very good, mostly out of date appliances and kitchenware, dumpy old furniture that smelled stale and yeasty. They had stacks and stacks of old books. On a whim, I bought a cardboard box full of them. The first few layers were all pulpy paperbacks—westerns and murder-by-numbers mystery series. At the very bottom were photo albums full of sepia-tinted pictures. Births and babies and arms caught in motion; blurs of activity, faces frozen halfway between laughter and tears.

I sat at the dinner table with those albums, engrossed in the images of strangers experiencing unknown lives. Our bird chirped beside me in his cage, bottom desperately in need of cleaning, full of broken seeds and bits of bird shit. I took the newer photos from their plastic sleeves and held them close to my face, absorbing details. I determined when the photos were taken by the style of clothes and hair, hem lengths—below or above the knee? The easiest to date were the Polaroids, warped like wet wood.

"Who's that? Your family?"

Elizabeth stood behind me holding milk gone warm, a white line circling the top of the glass from where it filmed over.

I didn't own pictures of myself as a kid. There was nothing showcasing little me with teeth too big for my mouth, sporting weird bowl haircuts or fringed bangs. In the album there were photographs of cookouts and Christmases and snapshots of suburban life, charming greeting card fodder. At the top of the stack sat a picture of a young woman with dark hair in a long braid. She looked solemn and pretty. Pale eyes, maybe blue or gray or green.

"My mother," I said, though my own mother was squat and tan with hair the color of dirty pennies. I circled the unfamiliar face with a fingertip, imagined her smoothing back my hair and fixing me breakfast: oatmeal, maybe, or waffles with syrup filling up every square.

"You look alike." Elizabeth kissed the back of my neck and I felt the milk on her lips leave a print. "Tell me about her."

The woman in the blue print dress held a big basket of laundry on her hip. She looked like the kind of mother who'd help with homework and pass candy out to trick-or-treaters. My own family never celebrated Halloween.

"She hated the taste of stale bread. Her favorite book was *The Black Stallion*, but she only ever read it twice because she didn't want to ruin the magic. She knew how to French braid hair."

Elizabeth sat beside me as I flipped through the album. She hooked her fingers around my wrist, nails slid gently along my skin. They scratched in soothing counterpoint to my pulse.

Top Right Corner, Fourth Page:

A woman sat at a big table shelling peas, surrounded by stacks of folded linens. Her hair was piled on the top of her head, a clean expanse of the kitchen visible behind her.

"We had a big Sunday dinner every week, the whole extended family."

My own mother never made a family meal beyond spaghetti or tuna casserole, but she'd liked to buy dessert mixes. There were boxes of Jell-O 1-2-3 stashed in our cupboards that had to be thrown out after they'd clumped into solid fruit-flavored bricks.

Middle Section, Bottom Left Page:

A woman's hair burned copper in the glare of the sun next to a too-blue swimming pool, swimsuit a limp green bikini that sags at the rear. A little boy stood next to her with his hand wrapped around her thigh. He wore too-small trunks, dark hair plastered to his forehead. He frowned, almost a grimace.

"My cousin almost drowned in that pool."

We'd had a slip and slide that sat sentient in the middle of our yard for over three years, filled with mildewed green water and then with baby tadpoles. I'd cupped mounds of them with my bare hands. My cousins were all at least ten years younger than me. I didn't know them at all, outside of baptisms and forced family birthday parties where they cried and smeared cake across their fat cheeks.

Elizabeth's arm folded beneath mine as I flipped the pages; skin smooth and cool as my stories picked up steam. Pictures of the woman in her car, windows rolled down and big black sunglasses on. Two small children peering from the back seat.

"Roadtrip to The Grand Canyon. My mom packed all of our clothes in one suitcase."

Before I'd left home, I'd never ventured outside the state. My mother never left.

Later I stood outside in the dying June wind and let the breeze sweep beneath my sleep shorts. Our yard was a barren wasteland and the plants were all dying. My shadow sat beside another shadow, but longer, thinner. My imagined mother two steps behind me. The moss swayed violently in the oaks as the lake rippled like crushed velvet.

When I went back inside, I hid the albums in a plastic bin where we stored all our wrapping paper and gift bags, stuffing it to the back of the closet.

There were bits of flotsam filling up the corner of every room, things that needed to be attached with pliers or nails or a "Philips head," which meant a starburst shape that bit into a screw. There were bookshelves waiting to be installed in the front room, a closet organizer in pieces on the floor of our master closet, two giant baskets of clean laundry that I kept digging through instead of putting away.

The violets out front withered into crinkled brown lizard bodies. I bought new plants that fried up and died, tendrils outstretched in the dirt as if they were reaching to the neighbors for help. I brought home bags of fertilizer, special mixes and herbaceous greens, cedar mulch that smelled like the inside of a closet. I watered the plants less—I watered them more. Everything led to the same results: dry tumbleweeds that rolled through the bahiagrass. The dirt was gray and unforgiving, unless it rained. Then the yard became a mudslide that slunk out into the street and colored our driveway.

"You have a black thumb," Elizabeth said. She picked up a hanging pot of what should've been periwinkles. They'd dried to crisps, leaves shedding onto the floor.

I wiped my hand across Elizabeth's ass and left a dark handprint on her white shorts.

"And you have a dirty ass."

She dumped the dirt down the front of my shirt and we ran screaming through the yard like little kids. Her face was stretched from smiling and it was the first time in a while that I had stopped seeing her as the sticking jamb in the doorway, the encumbrance that wouldn't let me get things closed properly.

That night we sat in our living room in the same chair, legs pretzeled together as we watched an old movie. We shared one sweaty glass of iced tea, passing it back and forth until the drips of condensation dotted our shirts. Our hands made shadow shapes on the dim walls and on each other's thighs.

The phone rang the next day: my brother on the other end. I hadn't spoken to him since the last funeral. He told me my father died and that I needed to fly home. His voice was shaky and higher than I remembered, oddly formal, like he wasn't sure how I'd take the news. I didn't know how to tell him the news felt like nothing to me, that it felt like a stranger telling me a story about someone I'd never heard of before.

I told Elizabeth one of my Uncles died and I needed to attend the funeral out of state.

"How long will you be gone?"

She put her hand on my sleeve, plucking at the cuff, but she didn't look at my face—she looked past me to the backyard, like she was already thinking what she'd do around the house without me there to deter her.

"Probably a week."

"Yeah, okay."

I ran my fingertip along the downy hair at the side of her face. I kissed her there impulsively, a sticky smack. The bird twitted at us in his cage, annoyed by my random act of PDA. A bird hit the glass over our heads while I held her in my arms, startling us apart. I pulled out my suitcase from the spare bedroom closet while she got the shovel.

I left early, Elizabeth still wrapped in the sheets with one arm draped across my side of the bed, coveting the remaining warmth. I kissed the soft patch on the inside of her arm and made coffee for the road. Clouds hovered low in the sky, fat with humidity. I put the air conditioning on full blast so I wouldn't fall asleep, hands so cold that they shivered on the steering wheel. The talk radio station had on a woman who claimed to be a pet psychic. People called in and she talked in a brusque, no-nonsense voice. She made them put their pets on the phone—one woman's English bulldog panted hard enough into the receiver to be an obscene caller.

"Definitely depressed. He needs a creative outlet."

Though I wanted to stay by myself, I knew I'd be expected to stay with one of my aunts. The drive in was unsettling. Everything felt too familiar, the remembered ache of a broken bone. The ground flew by under the wheels of the car and I counted the number of times I spotted a stray dog, numbering the cars with Dixie flying in their back windows. The front of my Aunt Diane's house was littered with the remnants of old glass soda bottles that she'd tried to incorporate into a fence—she'd stuffed them neck-first into the dirt, and it could've been cute if half of them weren't broken.

My bedroom for the duration was on the back porch, half-enclosed by the ripped screen. A summer shower started up and rain wet the spread—a light mist like an amusement park ride. I kept my things stowed under the bed and fed the mosquitoes, slapping at them as they bloated on the bare skin of my arms and legs. My aunt moved back and forth in the kitchen. She had the television on and I heard the local news talking about a line of thunderstorms moving in from the western part of the state. Birds flew overhead in V-formation, and they looked like they were on the way back to my house. I wondered what Elizabeth was doing and when I called her she sounded out of breath.

"What are you up to?"

"Working."

I picked at the edge of the duvet. It had brown speckles at the lacy edges that would've bothered me at my own house, but felt perfectly normal for my family. It smelled like mothballs and cigarette smoke. The scent was balmy and comfortable, soothing like someone combing their fingers through my hair.

"Working on what?"

"Just projects."

That could've meant anything. I envisioned her repainting all the hallways, recovering the upholstery in busy fabrics. Moving all the furniture around so that when I got up in the middle of the night for a glass of water I'd trip over an ill-placed rug.

"How's the bird?" I asked.

"I dunno."

"Don't kill our pet."

"Amber, please." There was a pause, a purposeful readjustment of her tone. "How's everything going so far? Is the hotel okay?"

There was a hole in the screen porch, a round fissure by the foot of the daybed. A small trail of sugar ants wound their way past my dangling legs to congregate at a puddle of water underneath a plastic lawn chair.

"It's nice, there's a mini fridge."

We said goodbye and I told her I loved her. When I looked up, my aunt stood in the doorway, blocking the frame with her doughy body.

"Who was that?"

"A friend." It was said on autopilot, just like I would've said it to my own mother.

"We need to leave, get your purse."

I chain-smoked a pack of my aunt's cigarettes outside the funeral parlor. I hadn't smoked in years, but being around my family meant I drank more, swore more, smoked until my eyes blurred. When I walked back into the building, the air was thick with deodorized air sanitizer. I'd choked down two Xanax in the ladies room and everything had softened around the edges, downy as the curling slip of a felt blanket.

The officiating minister looked like he'd just managed to successfully grow facial hair. His voice warbled as he talked about my father's meaningful impact on the community. My brother sat across the room and we avoided eye contact. People got up to say a few words—men my father worked with, women from the church. None of my relatives.

"He was good at fixing cars." The man who spoke wore a white cowboy hat and his pants had grease on them. Probably one of my father's friends from the shooting range. He looked toward the closed casket like he could see inside, see the body. His eyes stayed wet and red. I couldn't even work up enough emotion to fake a sniffle.

Watching the man openly weep, I had a memory of riding shotgun in my father's truck. We were on our way to drop off a load of garbage at the dump. The day had been pleasant and cool. We'd joked around, singing loudly to country music, windows rolled down. His voice was surprisingly high and clear, a really sweet tenor. I'd laughed at something and then picked my nose, and that's when my father slapped the hell out of my thigh. The transition from happy to angry was sudden, how many of our interactions functioned.

Supper was served on the lawn outside my family's church. Flies buzzed the coleslaw and biscuits. There were congealing plates of fried chicken and tray after tray of macaroni and cheese with buttery bread croutons, my father's favorite. I ate everything. My stomach adapted quickly, remembering how to behave. The food functioned as a sedative. All I wanted to do was take a nap.

After two more helpings, I loaded up a to-go plate and drove to my parents' house. My brother was executor of the estate, but I'd been asked to look over my father's things, see if there was anything that I'd like to keep before the relatives ransacked it. My brother's selections were piled in boxes next to the front door. He'd picked through my father's cache of weaponry, hunting knives, guns, the old boxing gloves he used to put on us when I was young enough to play like a little man.

I went into the bedroom he shared with my mother for thirty years. Old beer steins sat on the dresser where he stored pennies for rolling and a wooden elephant figurine from Taiwan perched beside it, a good luck charm rubbed shiny. There was a picture of my grandmother when she was younger than me, a pin-up in a polka dot bathing suit. At the way-back of the top drawer I found a plastic pillbox full of our old baby teeth. The discovery left a fat lump in my throat. My father, the tooth fairy.

The teeth I kept along with the picture. As I left the house, I took deep breaths of my father: motor oil and musk, leftover beer, newsprint, cut grass. I understood that I did not know him and he did not know me, and that we'd never know each other. I wondered if he and my mother felt that way about their marriage. I thought that maybe Elizabeth didn't know me, and that maybe she didn't really want to, or maybe she just couldn't. The longer we knew each other the more we invented our history. The Elizabeth I lived with wasn't who I fell in love with, but I loved the new Elizabeth too—how she didn't brush her hair, the smell of her neck when it got sweaty and she hadn't taken a shower. How did you reconcile loving two different versions of a person?

I spent the drive home calculating the number of birds that might have hit the house—three a day times four days equaled an entire colony of birds murdered by plate glass. I wondered if Elizabeth buried them or left them to rot in the sun. If she gave our bird the grass seed he liked. If she'd gone to the store to get milk for my cereal.

When I pulled up the driveway her car was gone. She'd left the recycling bins at the curb again and the pickup was two days prior. I dragged them up to the house, rainwater and leftover remnants of beer spilling on my feet. The smell was pungent and yeasty. I kicked my shoes off in the doorway and walked inside in soggy socks.

Our bird was alone in Elizabeth's studio, propped against the wall by the mural, colors swirled and terrible. The lone remainder of sunshine paint sat high on the wall, a round and sickly sun. The bird's cage sat directly below it. He huddled at the very bottom corner, water bottle dumping drops on his head every few seconds. When I tapped at the bars, he ignored me. His feathers were prickled and patchy from where he'd obsessively groomed himself. The water was full and so were the seeds, but I couldn't help thinking that he was starved for affection. I decided to let him go. Outside, free, instead of stuck inside with us.

I carried the cage out past the piled boxes and bags of things that hadn't been unpacked. When the door opened to the backyard, the scent of rotten things hit me, sickly-sweet as vomit. I threw open the cage and the bird fell out, lying there lumped. At first he struggled and flopped, wings flicking up dirt from the lawn that never rooted grass. Then he managed to right himself. He took off awkwardly, lilting upwards into the branches of the arching oaks. Wild birds circled his flight pattern. His wings spread, suddenly graceful as he soared upward, then catching the breeze and swooping down. I stood at the back of the yard as he slammed into the plate glass, landing in the dirt beneath the window.

From my vantage point, I saw why the birds kept crashing into our home. It wasn't a house to them. It was a mirror: an expanse of green trees and blue sky, the sun a gleaming, buttery reflection of itself. It's only when I walked closer to where our bird lay broken on the ground that I finally saw Elizabeth's mural. She'd painted our finch over the smeary sunshine of wall. The streaks were feathered perfectly around the orange swirl of his cheek, the brown striations of head, the sharp beak. I struggled to understand how I could've missed it for so long: our shared bird on our shared wall in our shared home. The bird's wet black eye stared down at me as I grabbed the shovel from the garage, placing our nameless pet in the shallow grave alongside his kin.

See also: A history of glassmaking

Condensation puddles on the desk beneath an orange Gatorade bottle that Patricia will never drink. *Did you know that a nineteenth century decanter is more fragile than an old newspaper clipping?* Typing one handed, her thumb taps the screen of her phone while the other mops at the water. She rubs her palm against her polyester skirt, and then tries to dry it on the stretchy knit of her tights. *Did you know glass forms in nature when lightning strikes sand?*

Overhead the AC kicks on, beating at the air like an industrial white noise machine, bass thrum lulling her to a drowsy half-consciousness. What keeps her awake is the clamminess of her basement office and a bottomless mug of coffee, the remnants of cups past pooling oily contamination across its dark surface. Patricia stopped adding creamer two months ago after she realized that she'd gained fifteen pounds from all the fat and sugar; one teaspoon was a serving size, and she'd been drinking at least four of those in every cup. That's what the Gatorade is for, to keep her hydrated, but it's always just a little too salty.

There's a lightning stab behind her left eye from what's probably the start of a caffeine headache mixed with the glare from the computer screen and her spreadsheets. She takes off her glasses and scrubs at her face, but her hands are still damp and she feels her eye makeup smear beneath her fingertips. A bottle of Advil sits at the bottom of her purse, but she decides to wait on that for later; her headaches have been the only thing that's punctured the silence.

"We're going by Palmano's for pastries, you want anything?" Her supervisor Brad leans in through her office door. He looks like half a mannequin with his stark black hair combed over and shellacked.

She shakes her head, but he's already gone before he can see the smile that she'd tried to work up for him, to show that she might not want the company, but she at least appreciates the effort.

Some of the moisture has soaked into her paperwork and the ink is running a pale blue watercolor stain toward the center of the metadata—cataloging records with titles still unattached. *Did you know aluminosilicate glass makes up the materials of boats and halogen bulbs?*

When the AC kicks off again, Patricia looks at the clock. It's eleven in the morning, though there aren't any windows for her to see outside and look at what the weather might be like. She puts away her phone and decides to take an early lunch.

Though the work is tedious, Patricia enjoys her job. She's a records management administrator, which is just a fancy way of saying data entry technician. This sorting and sifting of random content comes easy to her, and it's a comfort to keep track of the minutiae. She likes the planner she keeps tucked in her bag, and her home calendar is synced with her work calendar, though most of her "home" appointments are just vet visits for the dog and biannual dental cleanings. For the last few months she's been weeding through the foundation's large collection of glass research and criticism. It's nice to think about the complexities of a substance she's never before considered.

Glass is one of those things that make up large portions of our lives, but we never actually notice it. She sits outside by the lake to eat lunch and lets her hands defrost while she picks the crust from her sandwich, piling it in a messy stack. *How many types of glass do we have in our homes? How much of it do we carry on our bodies?*

Turtles break the smooth, clean surface of the water into larger concentric rings that spread and lap at the shore. Trios clump in the shallows near the bench where she plays with her food. The air smells like mildew and crushed grass and the air is cold and damp. Everything's gray, including the sky. Her heels mark divots next to a big pile of fire ants. When an angry swarm of them marches too close to her foot, she gets up from the bench.

Patricia walks to the water's edge, dumping the crust into the lake and dusting off her hands until the crumbs and seeds fly free. Whole-wheat bread was on sale last week at the grocery store, buy-one-get-one-free, and she couldn't get herself to buy the kind she actually liked in favor of the value. The dark bread is hard and nutty and already stale. Patricia misses when everything came on white bread and was easier to chew. The turtles scramble awkwardly toward her. They know who she is. Their heads shoot out of the water as they lurch gracelessly over each other to reach the scraps. Patricia finds them simultaneously ugly and adorable, like the old men in their cardigans and high-necked sweaters who argue with each other over chess in the park by her house.

There's the sharp sound of a car door slamming. Her coworkers are back from their excursion—they're climbing out of a silver Ford across the parking lot. When they turn toward her, she adjusts her body so she's looking back out at the lake again, which has smoothed out into a mirror.

Glass blowing is something she's heard of but never seen or participated in. There are workshops nearby. Patricia thinks of all the objects one could make from blown glass. *What would happen if you inhaled during a glass blowing session? Would an x-ray show the fine, fragile coating of your esophagus?*

There's no reply to any of her texts, but she didn't really expect one.

Half her uneaten lunch goes back into a paper bag, which she crumples and throws into a nearby trashcan. Patricia flexes her fingers and wonders how much longer she can put off going home for the day.

Inside she sips her cold coffee and types up data reports one handed while she scrubs at her eyes, wipes at her peeling lipstick, scrubs at her eyes again. She has to wash her eyeglasses with dish soap when she's at home because the oil from her face will accumulate until even her eyelashes stick to the surface of the lens like small black commas.

"Any fun plans this weekend?" It's the other woman named Patricia. Actually, there are three of them in their office; it seems like most data systems women are called Patricia, as if they chose their line of work based off name alone. This one calls herself Patty. The other one calls herself Patti with an *i*. Patricia always fights to keep the whole name to herself—just Patricia, she'll say, I like the formality of it, or, it's a family name, even though nobody else is named Patricia in her family, at least not that she knows of.

"Just sleep," she says. She smiles and for a second it feels good, stretching out the unused muscles in her cheeks.

"I hear that." Patty has short hair, the kind that most catalogers wear; the kind she's seen in a meme on the internet called the "can I speak to a manager" haircut. Patricia refuses to cut her hair. She keeps it absurdly long, even though it gets in her face and bothers her and most days she just scrapes it back into a ponytail.

"Wanna come to happy hour with us?" Patty asks.

They ask her almost every other Friday. Patricia's always said no—not because she has other plans, but because she just can't see herself spending more time than she already does with these people. They share no interests, and Patricia's never been very social. But then her phone buzzes in her hand. She looks down at the screen, wondering if it's a reply, finally, after waiting what seems like years.

It's a coupon text from the fabric store where she bought yarn three months ago.

"I'd love to," Patricia says, and the surprised look on the other woman's face is enough to make her glad about her decision.

It's a Mexican restaurant that's not really a Mexican restaurant; more like a TGI Fridays that sells overpriced food that's trying too hard. Patricia's never been inside before, but she recognizes it immediately. She usually passes the place on her way home from work, stuffed into a dirty subdivision, sandwiched between a Staples office supply store and an out-of-business Kmart. It's the kind of place where they have posters on the ceiling and everything looks like it was last renovated in the eighties; Springsteen songs on the jukebox, laminate counters, and sticky floors that make traction difficult and make her wonder if someone spilled syrup. The smell of hot oil and corn chips from the back makes her stomach rumble in an embarrassing way. She's glad for the loud music.

All four of them are crammed together at a little round table at a back corner by the bar. The place is packed, mostly people drinking neon pitchers of urine-colored beer while a football game plays on the TV's that are anchored in every corner of the building.

When she orders her drink, she's got to scream at the waitress to be heard over the music and the guys cheering on the football players.

"Nachos," she yells, cupping a hand around her mouth. "And a Coke."

Patty digs an elbow into her side. "C'mon, don't make us look bad."

The waitress appears simultaneously bored and aggravated, even though she's smiling at them all. Her teeth are pretty, very even and shockingly white. She's young enough that she probably wishes she were out for the night and not working a shift that's going to make her hair smell like fried food.

"Whiskey and Coke," Patricia amends, and Patty's elbow finally leaves her ribcage.

There are two other women who sit with them, but Patricia doesn't know them very well. One works in the archives and the other is her supervisor's administrative assistant. She can only remember the admin's name, which is Beth, and that she just got engaged two weeks ago. There was an email chain that had gone around suggesting a bridal shower or office party, but Patricia had stopped opening those emails and just let them drift to the bottom of her queue.

They've ordered two pitchers of margaritas and their drinks are slopping onto the glass top of the table. Patricia puts her napkin in front of herself as a barricade in case one of the very full glasses decides to tip over on its spindly neck. The waitress brings over Patricia's drink and the platter of nachos. All of the women help themselves while Patricia sips at her drink, which tastes like whiskey and the smallest drip of Coke possible. She can't remember the last time she had anything stronger than white wine.

"Thanks, these are awesome." The woman from archives already has salsa on her chin.

"Yeah, these are the best." Beth takes a large portion and scoops it onto a plate in front of her. The nachos are dwindling rapidly. Patricia isn't sure what she's supposed to do with her hands or what she should say, so she takes another drink and lets the ice chill her teeth.

Did you know that in the 1800s glass bottles were mostly used for storing whiskey? Her fingers are numb against the screen on her phone. Beth has hers out too, probably texting her fiancé. She's very cute and young. She's got an asymmetrical black bob and wears a butter-colored silk dress with Manolo Blahniks. Patricia wonders how she can afford any of it on an admin salary.

Most of the chips are already gone and Patricia's only eaten two of them. None of the other women have ordered food and they don't seem like they're going to anytime soon. The drink hurts her stomach and sours her breath, making her wish for an antacid.

"I'm going to go get us more chips," Patricia says, but the three women are leaning in toward each other, heads like magnets, and something has happened on the TV overhead, someone's scored, and the loud yelling from the bar is enough to make her want to go out and sit in her car.

She waits behind a man in a faded polo shirt and a woman in a black strapless dress until she can squeeze her way up to the bar. The top is shiny and lacquered, and it feels cool against her hand. When she picks up her glass to show it to the waitress, she can see particles floating in the watered down liquid through the spotted sides of her highball.

"Another?" The waitress points at Patricia's drink while simultaneously pouring shots for the rowdy group of guys at the other end of the bar.

"Could I have more nachos for my table?" Patricia passes over the glass, then puts her hand up when the waitress takes it. "And just Coke this time."

The drink looks exactly how it will taste—sweet and fizzy enough to make her stomachache go away. The woman next to her is blonde and petite, smaller than Patricia, even though Patricia's barely five feet four. When Patricia takes a sip of her drink, the woman jostles her arm. Some of it spills down her cleavage and into her shirt, where it stains the white collar brown, close enough to match her coffee stains.

"Jesus, sorry!" The woman hands Patricia the napkin beneath her glass, which has the perfect circle of her daiquiri beneath it. She looks very neat and put together, with very nice matching pumps to go with her dress, and Patricia looks down at her olive cardigan and khaki skirt and wishes she'd thought to at least put on some more lipstick.

At the other side of the bar, Patricia spots Beth waiting for the single-stall restroom. One of the guys who's just finished his shot goes up to talk with her and Beth smiles the kind of smile that says thanks but please don't talk to me again. Even from across the room, Patricia can see the icy frost of her stare, but the man's eyes are glazed too, like they're coated with a thin sheen of oil. When the bathroom opens up, Beth scoots inside and Patricia goes back to her table.

"Did you get the nachos?" Patty asks. The plate in front of them is shockingly clean, and the other woman is actually scraping the burnt cheese bits off with her fork.

"They're on their way." Patricia drinks some more of her Coke and hopes her stomach settles.

There's a buzz from her pocket as the waitress arrives with another tray of loaded chips. *Why are you sending me this junk, Mom?*

"Could someone drive me home? I'm not feeling well." Beth's got one knee on her seat and one hand on her stomach, but her eye makeup is drippy in the corners and her nose is red.

"I can take you." Patricia throws some money on the table. This excuse to leave is as good as any. She doesn't wait for goodbyes or for anyone to follow her. When the cold air hits her face, she feels like she can finally breathe again.

In the car, she tunes the radio to a talk station. The volume's too low to hear what anyone's actually saying. Patricia isn't sure if Beth wants to talk, but she's not about to facilitate anything. Her own head is roiling.

"It's just all happening really fast," Beth's saying, and then everything is running out of this woman like steam from a kettle. "I wasn't even sure we should be dating and now we're engaged, and then two months from now we'll be married? And I'll have to live with him in his shitty duplex? Do you know that he's never even used an iron before?" Beth laughs and clutches her seatbelt as Patricia weaves them carefully in and out of traffic. The road is shiny and slick; it's started sprinkling, the kind of wet that makes the road turn into liquid ice. In Florida it hardly ever freezes, but the oil on the road after rain is slick enough to compensate for any lack of snow.

"I don't know how to use an iron." Patricia offers this like penance; there's lots of things she doesn't know how to do, things that she just thought she'd magically know by her forties.

"Have you ever been married?" Beth asks, suddenly, and Patricia is happy that she can answer this one question.

"Yes, but not for very long." She pauses. "It wasn't . . . right."

"See! This is exactly what I mean." Beth laughs. "Exactly."

Patricia's not sure what any of this could mean. Her marriage is something she views from very far away, like a story someone must have told her at a party. It's all very clichéd—she was young, he was young. They got pregnant. The marriage began and ended in the span of two years. She went off to pursue an internship abroad, thinking she'd become more worldly when really the opposite had happened. She'd come home from London and no longer knew her son, who toddled to his stepmother with a gummy grin never aimed Patricia's way. None of this she tells Beth, who digs through her purse, looking for gum.

Traffic lights blink through the windshield and the back window of the car in front of her, a Subaru hatchback, and then through *their* windshield. It's a fuzzy red glow through three separate sheets of tempered glass. The water turns it all into a haloed mess, speckling her hands with the same bright haze, illuminating the grooves on her knuckles—lines she'd once mistaken for dehydration. All the water in the world isn't going to get rid of them now.

"That guy, back at the bar, he said something to me."

"He was drunk," Patricia says, and then stops herself. She doesn't know this story and she shouldn't assume anything. "I'm sorry. What did he say?"

"He said, if your fiancé really loved you, then why wouldn't he be out with you tonight?" Beth laughs again, fiddling with the stereo knob, turning it up and down again. "Here's the thing, he did want to come out with me, I just didn't want to be around him! That's fucked. I know that's fucked."

"Is this your street?" Patricia puts on her turn signal, slowing down to brake before the street.

"Yeah, that little blue house on the corner, with the stones out front by the mailbox."

There's another car in the driveway, a Jeep with the windows out. The front porch light flicks on and the door opens to the front of the house, leaving whoever's standing there in shadow. The shape elongates to bat-like proportions, and then Patricia sees that it's just a man holding an umbrella.

Beth opens the car door and lets in a drizzle that leaks down into the seat. She slams it behind her, waving at Patricia through the speckled glass as the man meets her halfway down the driveway under the umbrella's black top. He waves too, and Patricia waves back.

She tunes the station to Christmas carols, one that plays them all December long. The speed limit is low, mostly residential streets, and only a few other cars are out. Everyone is driving like they've got no place special to be. There's only one main highway between her and home. She thinks about making a fire when she gets home, maybe sitting beside the tree.

Bing Crosby croons "Silver Bells" as she watches the traffic lights bounce off her windshield. It takes her a minute to realize that the odd noise she'd attributed to the radio is actually a voice. Someone's shouting and it's coming from the car idling directly to her right. From the corner of her eye she can tell that it's a black truck, one that stands several feet above her own small sedan, but there's something about the shouting—the way that the voice sounds overly loud and hoarse that lets her brain know she should just keep facing forward, that she should maybe sing along with the music on the radio, a duet with Bing, and ignore the person beside her. The shouting continues and she's stuck at the light, ignoring the man who's waving one long, pale arm that's so close to the glass of her passenger window that she's internally flinching.

As the song cuts to commercial, she can make out more of the words. She hears *Bitch* and *Cunt* mingled over an ad for a fifty-percent-off storewide mattress sale, and the talking dog sounds just like Scooby Doo. Mostly the man screams the word *Hey* repeatedly, as if she's just missed his voice before and the repetition will get her attention. It reminds her of the joke her father used to tell about "hay being for horses," and the thought makes a giggle choke deep in her throat and she has to focus on the steering wheel to stop herself from laughing, pulling at a loose thread that's popped up, wiping one finger down a slick place in the leather where she always likes to rest her hand at the very top of the wheel.

Her brain crawls over the facts: how fast she'd been driving down the six-lane highway that brackets Beth's house from her own, only really a ten-minute drive with just the one big road between them, whether she'd cut him off at a light or a turn, thinking backwards, quickly, scrambling over what she could have possibly done to make this man so angry with her that he'd scream profanity at a rolled up window. When the next song comes on, it's "Rockin' Around the Christmas Tree." She sings loudly along with it and wonders if the man can hear her through the opposite side of the glass.

A blue Toyota beside her does an illegal U-turn instead of waiting for the green arrow. She pulls her car into the turn lane and waits there for the light, even though it's going in the opposite direction of home. At least it puts a lane between them so that she won't be able to hear his voice any more.

But as she pulls into the lane, the truck moves into the spot that she's vacated. Now she's trapped, waiting for an arrow that she knows from experience takes at least five minutes to turn green. If anything, the man's voice has gotten shriller. Even though the words are garbled, the word *HEY* is there like a neon sign, pronounced in all capital letters. Patricia stares at the light through the back window of the car in front of her and wonders what she'll do if this man decides he wants to get out of his car. No one around her seems to hear anything through the thick glass of their own cars and trucks and SUVs and minivans. She's surrounded by a sea of people but completely alone, except for the Christmas music and the man from the truck who won't stop screaming.

Just as her arrow finally turns green, there's a sound like a dropped plate. She actually sees it before she hears it; the man has flung a handful of loose change at the side of her car, hitting the window with such force that she's afraid the glass will break. Her sweaty hands slip along the steering wheel as she turns down the street toward the parking lot of a nearby grocery store. At least the lights will be on there. At least there will be security guards and people to see her, maybe help if the man follows her.

She pulls into the lot and then noses the car into the first available space, which is next to a young woman settling her kid into a car seat. Patricia sits there with the radio still blasting Christmas music. The woman beside her makes eye contact and gives a thumbs up—everyone loves "All I Want for Christmas is You."

Patricia climbs out into the cold air. The burn feels good against her face and her sweaty neck. The woman beside her tugs her hair into a ponytail and Patricia can hear the little boy yelling through the closed door of the car as he bangs his small, sticky fist against the glass. The woman smiles tiredly at Patricia and it's like she's seeing her past self there in the parking lot, exhausted and overwhelmed, looking out at the world like she's trapped inside a dirty snow globe that's slowly drying up inside.

"Happy holidays," the woman says, and throws the pink hood of her sweatshirt over her head, jamming her hands into the pockets. There's a dark loop of hair curling out of the side, and Patricia wants to smooth it back for the woman, tell her that it's going to get better. "My kid is teething. Isn't that the best Christmas gift ever?"

"It'll pass," Patricia says. "It always does."

As the woman pulls out of the lot, Patricia walks stiffly around her car, her legs like stilts inside her pants, checking to see if her lights aren't working, or if her trunk has somehow come open. Anything to warrant the man yelling at her, trying to make sense of the nonsense that likely had nothing to do with Patricia at all.

There are scuff marks in the silver paint of her passenger door, but she can't tell if they're from whatever the man threw at her car or just regular wear and tear. She climbs back into the passenger seat and drives home to "Frosty the Snowman" and "Deck the Halls," and Nat King Cole sings the "Christmas Song" while her heart still tries to slow its beat to a respectable rhythm. This time she doesn't sing along.

Something's knocked over the paper kindling she's set aside in the backyard for a fire. She crouches to collect it while the dog, Sally, takes her time poking around, sniffing at some of the poinsettias that

Patricia was gifted at work last week. They're already withering; a pile of red leaves circle the pots.

"Sally, get back from there." She can't remember if poinsettia is poisonous to animals. Her dog is her longest-held companion—a twelve-year-old golden retriever mix. Her coat is graying in the face and the chest in a way that Patricia thinks looks scholarly. Sometimes she'll tug Sally's chin hair and call her Professor Dog.

When she whistles for Sally, the dog ignores her. Her hearing's mostly gone. Patricia can yell her name in the same room and the dog won't turn around. Sally's rump is in the air as she pushes into a bush, probably checking out whatever animal knocked over the kindling. Patricia rubs her arms and shivers. She's still shaking from the interaction with the man, even though she's convinced herself almost that it never happened, that maybe it's just a nightmare she had that's dissipating on waking. She leaves Sally outside and goes to change into her sleep shirt, the one with the high neck and flannel flower print that feels fuzzy between her fingers.

In her kitchen she puts on the silver kettle, waiting for her ancient stovetop to heat it to a boiling point. She unearths a pack of Sleepytime tea from the back of her cupboard. It's so old that the bags have turned a little brown and lost most of their scent, but her stomach is still unsettled and it seems like her best option.

There's a sharp bang on the sliding glass door. Boiling tea slips over the rim of her mug as she jumps. The liquid slides down her hand and into her sleeve, leaving a burning trail that stains her skin bright red.

Sally's at the sliding door, paws pressed to the glass. She jumps, banging into it over and over, as if she can run straight through into the living room. Patricia slides the door open and the dog spills inside, a high whine curling from her throat and sliding into Patricia's ears. She crouches on the ground with the dog, who's rubbing her head and face all over Patricia's stomach. Patricia cries in genuine alarm, unsure how to help. She remembers when she'd gotten the dog, with her son Marcus, for his tenth birthday, as a gift to make up for all the times she'd been absent from his life—the baseball games she'd missed, the times she hadn't been there to help with his math homework. Her son, dark haired and lovely, knelt on the ground outside a cage filled with puppies. His pants had gotten filthy from the concrete and the pee stains and all the dog hair piled up like dust bunnies.

"This one," he'd said, as Sally crawled into his lap, snuggling down into the safety of her little boy's stocky frame. "This one's my buddy."

They'd brought that wriggling yellow body back to Patricia's apartment, and Marcus had seemed less sad. She'd felt closer to him than she had in years, ever since she'd given up primary custody of him in favor of her ex-husband and his new wife, who both made three times as much money as she did.

Patricia sits down on the couch and helps Sally crawl up beside her, staring at the reflection of her Christmas tree in the sliding glass door. She remembers what it felt like to hold her baby one night beneath the glow of a very different tree, the two of them lying together on their ratty old blue and white plaid couch. It had been so cold in that apartment—they were both wearing coats, counting down to midnight on her twentieth birthday. How she'd held Marcus, his skull soft and fragile in the palm of her hand, watching his eyes glow under the white Christmas lights. It had made her feel small and large at the same time.

After leaving her husband and her son, her mother had called and berated her for nearly an hour. "What kind of a mother are you?" she'd asked, over and over again. Patricia didn't know how to answer that. She still doesn't.

In the silence of the room, she can hear her own breath mingled with the heavy snuffling of the dog. Patricia grabs her phone off the coffee table and pulls Sally close to her, snapping a picture of the two of them. The tree glows in the background, haloing both of their faces. Sally looks angelic, her hair a white halo around her large head. She sends the picture to her son, halfway across the country in college. Then she wipes the smudges from the screen with the tail of her sleep shirt and drinks the rest of her tea.

Acknowledgments

"Biddenden Maids" was first published at *North American Review*

"Felt in the Jaw" was first published at OSU's *The Journal*

"The Locusts" was first published at *Hawaii Pacific Review*

"Playing Fetch" was first published at *The Normal School*

"A Decline in Natural Numbers" was first published at *Pithead Chapel*

"Notice of a Fourth Location" was first published at *Joyland Magazine*

"See also: A history of glassmaking" was first published in *Ninth Letter* as the 2015 Fiction Award Winner

NOW AVAILABLE FROM

Split Lip Press

9 781974 186044

ML OCT 2019